Aphorism in the Francophone Novel of the Twentieth Century

In this exploration of twentieth-century novels written in French, Mark Bell defines aphorism as a literary genre and demonstrates how it is used in seven texts that provide a cross-section of ideological stances and francophone communities.

Aphorism in the Francophone Novel of the Twentieth Century includes critical readings of *Terre des hommes* by Antoine de Saint-Exupéry, *Alexandre Chenevert* by Gabrielle Roy, *Gouverneurs de la rosée* by Jacques Roumain, *Pluie et vent sur Télumée miracle* by Simone Schwarz-Bart, *La route des Flandres* by Claude Simon, *Présence de la mort* by C.F. Ramuz, and *Neige noire* by Hubert Aquin. Bell addresses the problems inherent in the term aphorism, the narrative and discourse function of aphorism within the genre of the novel, the interrelation between the structure of aphorism and the epistemological and hermeneutical functions this sub-genre may perform as a component part of the narrative fabric, the "national" character of aphoristics, and the problems that arise from "anthologizing" a novel's aphorisms.

The importance of aphoristic formulation in the French literary tradition and its undeniable presence in the modern novel make this a particularly significant and fruitful study.

MARK BELL is assistant professor of French, Brigham Young University.

Aphorism in the Francophone Novel of the Twentieth Century

MARK BELL

McGill-Queen's University Press
Montreal & Kingston • London • Buffalo

© McGill-Queen's University Press 1997
ISBN 0-7735-1528-3

Legal deposit second quarter 1997
Bibliothèque nationale du Québec

Printed in Canada on acid-free paper

Published simultaneously in the European Union by
Liverpool University Press.

Funding for the manuscript has been received from the
Brigham Young University College of Humanities.

Canadian Cataloguing in Publication Data

Bell, Mark, 1951–
    Aphorism in the Francophone novel of the twentieth
    century
    Includes bibliographical references and index.
    ISBN 0-7735-1528-3
    1. French literature – 20th century – History and
    criticism. 2. Aphorisms and apothegms in literature.
    I. Title.
    PQ673.B44 1997   843'.91091   C96-900871-6

Typeset in Palatino 10/12
by Caractéra inc., Quebec City

Contents

1 Introduction 3

2 Aphorism in Twentieth-Century Narrative Prose in French: Theoretical Considerations 7

3 *Terre des hommes* 37

4 *Alexandre Chenevert* 50

5 *Gouverneurs de la rosée* 62

6 *Pluie et vent sur Télumée Miracle* 71

7 *La Route des Flandres* 79

8 *Présence de la mort* 93

9 *Neige noire* 101

10 Conclusion 111

   APPENDICES

A *Terre des hommes* 119

B *Alexandre Chenevert* 124

C *Gouverneurs de la rosée* 130

D *Pluie et vent sur Télumée Miracle* 134

E *La Route des Flandres* 136

vi   Contents

F   *Présence de la mort*   141

G   *Neige noire*   143

References   147

Index   151

Aphorism in the Francophone Novel of the Twentieth Century

1 Introduction

This study explores how francophone authors use aphorism in seven novels published in the twentieth century. To be more exact, we will consider how writers conceive their own aphorisms and incorporate them into a novel's narrated chain of events.

No substantial investigation of aphorism in the contemporary French-language novel has been undertaken to date. Therefore, as a point of departure it seems advisable to take into account two seminal studies before embarking on such a project.

Jefferson Humphries, in *The Puritan and the Cynic: Moralists and Theorists in French and American Letters* (1987), focuses on aphorism in seventeenth-century French prose and in modern French poetry. He also articulates a rationale of "commonplace" utterances, invoking mainly deconstructionist assumptions. As a result of his inquiry Humphries posits the survival of the "maxim," at least in modern French poetry, as "a sort of negation of itself" (viii). While this premise may apply to some sententious formulation in French novels written in the twentieth century, it proves inadequate to a host of other texts. However, the idea is useful, restrictive as it might be, for it prompts more extensive inquiry into the ways that aphorism contributes to overall meaning in the novel.

The second study, *Sententiousness and the Novel: Laying down the Law in Eighteenth-Century French Fiction* by Geoffrey Bennington (1985), is helpful for the way it exposes the gamut of problems we encounter when we consider aphoristic propositions within imaginative prose. In a "postscript" that acts as an *hors texte* Bennington claims not to have drawn any conclusions. Instead, he invites further investigation that would serve to amplify his sparse but none the less incisive demarcations of each issue. He explains: "I have tried to avoid totalization, be it that of a narrative of the 'eighteenth century' inserted into some notional 'history of sententiousness' ... or of some conclusive theoretical statement. No final sententious 'thesis of the thesis.' But it is still perhaps possible to look proleptically towards further work, to local testings and modifications of the gestures elaborated here" (209).

Like Humphries, Bennington limits his investigation to a distinct period, in this case eighteenth-century French fiction. He suggests, perhaps somewhat reductively, that aphorism in the novel of that period performed a sententious function – a "laying down of the law," as it were. Working from this assumption, Bennington then critiques the didactic, totalizing use of aphorism from a post-structuralist perspective, relying particularly on the deconstructionist notion of indeterminacy. Again, such a confined approach turns out to be inadequate to account for the complexities of aphorism in the contemporary French-language novel.

The objective of the initial, theoretical section of the present study is to build on the foundation that Bennington and Humphries have laid. To accomplish this task, I draw upon a well-developed body of German scholarship in an attempt to define the genre as thoroughly as possible. Next, the work of several linguists and theorists active in North America – notably William Labov, Paul Hopper, and Kenneth Burke – help to establish the function of aphorism within a narrated chain of events. My decision to choose these theorists' approaches over so many other possible ones is governed by their seminal nature and by their relative lack of extraneous, complicating factors.

Finally, it seems profitable to consider Paul Ricoeur's revisiting of traditional hermeneutics. His work helps to establish a possible link between aphorism as a highly concentrated expression of thought and the bearing this genre might have on a reader's reception of a novel as a whole.

Thus, the following fundamental issues will first be addressed in the theoretical section and will then reappear with particular reference to each novel:

- the problems inherent in the term *aphorism*;
- the narrative and discourse function of aphorism within the genre of the novel;
- the interrelation between the structure of aphorisms and the epistemological and hermeneutical functions this subgenre might perform as a component part of the narrative fabric;

- the "national" character of aphoristics: i.e., might an idiosyncratically French (versus, for example, a German) variant of the phenomenon exist?
- the problems that arise from "anthologizing" a novel's aphorisms; put differently, what occurs when aphoristic sentences are read in isolation from their original co-text?

It seemed advisable to limit the selection of novels considered in such a study to widely known texts taken from several "national" bodies of literature. Thus, classics from the French, Québécois, *négro-africain*, and Swiss canons will form the basis for analysis.

The internal sequencing of the seven novels is governed by a hypothetical continuum of aphoristic "intervention." At one end of such a continuum are texts where the author conspicuously and often didactically stops the narrative momentum to interpose aphoristic commentary. At the other are placed "new" and postmodern narratives, which integrate subjective intrusion with greater subtlety. Each of the seven novels might serve as a paradigm and thus represent, roughly, a point on the proposed continuum.

Finally, the study will frequently shift from structural analysis to interpretation, or to "the world" that a given text might be seen to project. So, in selecting a sample of novels for the study, I attempt to account for a wide variety of ideological groundings: a Nietzschean, elitist humanism in Saint-Exupéry's *Terre des hommes* (1939); a modest humanism in Gabrielle Roy's *Alexandre Chenevert* (1955); a Marxist-utopian perspective in Jacques Roumain's *Gouverneurs de la rosée* (1946). Simone Schwarz-Bart, in her *Pluie et vent sur Télumée Miracle* (1972), features "new historicist" concerns of race, gender, and class. Claude Simon's "nouveau roman" *La Route des Flandres* (1960) constitutes a highly idosyncratic view of how consciousness and memory might be re-presented in written texts. C.F. Ramuz was one of the first non-French authors to resist the tyranny he perceived the French literary elite to exercise. Taking the painter Cézanne as a model, Ramuz also sought to inscribe a metaphysical vision in which the author is both present and constantly seen to withdraw. The pivotal *Présence de la mort* (1922) will represent all of Ramuz's production, which defies easy classification. Last, I will consider a postmodern, overtly reader-oriented (and therefore supposedly indeterminate) novel: Hubert Aquin's *Neige noire* (1977).

An appendix to each of the novels is included for the purpose of quick reference. Any fragment from the entire text that might be construed as an aphorism is listed in the appendix. The underlying rationale for creating such a listing is explained in the next chapter.

Suffice it to say that at times, for reasons of economy and smooth flow, a given aphorism is only partially quoted within the body of the study. The more complete text can readily be consulted in the corresponding appendix.

Finally, throughout the text the term "francophone" will apply in its broad connotation, as opposed to the more narrow one of "outside metropolitan France." Michel Tétu insists on this wider definition in the influential *La Francophonie*. Likewise, including France in the list of francophone countries is the *modus operandi* of the Conseil International d'Etudes Francophones.

2 Aphorism in Twentieth-Century Narrative Prose in French: Theoretical Considerations

In reading Mme de Lafayette's *La Princesse de Clèves*, written during the period when the French *moralistes* were publishing many volumes of sententious formulations, we should not be surprised to encounter such propositions as "Les paroles les plus obscures d'un homme qui plaît donnent plus d'agitation que les déclarations ouvertes d'un homme qui ne plaît pas" (294). For a moment this sentence, cast suddenly in the present tense rather than in the *passé simple*, interrupts the narrative flow and calls attention to itself.

What, however, are we to think of such interventions in the case of twentieth-century narrative prose? For example, how might we assess the function of the terse pronouncements that Sartre regularly interposes as the narrative of *La Nausée* progresses? A single example suffices to illustrate: "jamais un existant ne peut justifier l'existence d'un autre existant" (247).

Further, how might aphorisms such as the following, which appear respectively in novels by Proust, Colette, and Gide, bear upon the overall discourse of the novel, and upon the reader's reception of it?

notre personnalité sociale est une création de la pensée des autres. Même l'acte si simple que nous appelons "voir une personne que nous connaissons" est en partie un acte intellectuel. (*Swann* 18–19)

Pour écrire un livre il faut de la patience, et aussi pour apprivoiser un homme en état de sauvagerie, et pour raccommoder du linge usé, et pour trier les raisins de Corinthe destinés au plum-cake. (*Naissance du jour* 110)

Combien d'affirmateurs doivent leur force à cette chance de n'avoir pas été compris à demi-mot!   (*L'Immoraliste* 167)

As we observe such aphoristic texts, do they in any way distinguish themselves from those found in other national literatures? Put more specifically, might we observe anything particularly "French" about their constitution? And finally, to what extent are aphorisms such as these capable of standing by themselves? What of an independent existence – a genre unto themselves – in a separate anthology?

APHORISM AND ITS NEIGHBORING TERMINOLOGIES: "A WILDERNESS OF DEFINITIONS"

The term used throughout this study, *aphorism*, warrants a thorough-going preliminary discussion because of its problematic nature. The decision in favour of this term over other related ones must be taken advisedly, for one is confronted in the relevant literature with a wide range of possibilities: proverb, epigram, the commonplace, maxim, dictum, sentence, sententiousness, sententious proposition, axiom, precept, law, slogan, apothegm, proverbial locution, adage, generics, fragment, *devise*, and bonmot. Even this lengthy enumeration consti-tutes only an incomplete list of all the terminology that borders on *aphorism*.

   François Rodegem, in "Un problème de terminologie: les locutions sentencieuses," goes so far as to propose a taxonomic matrix in an attempt to define and categorize definitively the various terms. Bennington points out how Rodegem's criteria encompass an unwieldy array of concepts – for instance, "rhythm," "metaphoric-ity," and "normative thrust." Bennington reveals the pitfalls inherent in such a taxonomy of sententiousness and warns of "the danger of assuming that sententious discourse can be thought of as a unified 'space' adequately covered by the terms available for designating individual sententious utterances, and the consequent apriorism implicit in the assumption that each of the available terms must correspond to a distinct position in the matrix" (11). For this reason Bennington opts in his study for the broader term "sententiousness." Nevertheless, even this word carries with it a semantic load that severely limits the scope and function of "generic" (aphoristic) formulation within imaginative prose. The notion of sententiousness, or as Bennington recasts it, a "laying down of the law," may well apply to the bulk of eighteenth-century French fiction – and both Bennington and Humphries argue this point convincingly – but what of literary texts in post-Nietzschean Western civilization? While it is true that the "sententious" novel of the eighteenth century is an impelling ancestor of the twentieth-century francophone novel, one must ask whether the idea of "laying down the law" accurately applies to the diversity of aphoristic phenomena we encounter in it.

Four otherwise disparate pieces of scholarship cast some clarifying light on what John Gross aptly refers to as "a wilderness of definitions" (vii). These four pieces complement and at times corroborate one another; the common space they occupy stems from the fact that they all posit the appropriateness of the terms "aphorism," "aphoristic," and "aphoristics" to denote the phenomenon that forms the object of this study. The four studies in question, especially those of Bennington and Humphries, are close to one another in their dates of publication. Enough time has elapsed since this flurry of activity to evaluate them as a kind of composite entity and elaborate upon them.

In *Linguistics and the Novel* Roger Fowler offers a concise point of departure for a preliminary discussion of aphorism within narrative prose. Fowler takes elements from Fielding's *Tom Jones* to illustrate his hypothesis that "'Fielding' doesn't hesitate to announce directly his views on the ethics of human behavior ... by proclamations of general moral 'truths.' The latter may be announced in the form of aphoristic generic sentences. These are very recognizable semi-proverbial sentences in which the speaker asserts the truth of the predicate in respect of all possible referents of the subject noun phrase. Such sentences are typically cast in the 'timeless' present tense" (86). Fowler tends here to combine somewhat indiscriminately the notions of proverb and aphorism, thereby illustrating a problem of terminology that must eventually be confronted. His comments are valuable at this introductory stage, however, for they neatly formulate the concept of "aphoristic generic sentences" and their fusion to the novelistic genre.

Further, Fowler demonstrates how authors frequently devise "transformational disguises" to "avoid the alienating dogmatism of the explicit form of the generic" (87). This means that instead of employing within the narrative fully formed aphorisms capable of standing alone, authors may choose to embed them in the deep structure of the text. To illustrate, Fowler continues to employ material from *Tom Jones*: "For instance, what reader but knows that Mr Allworthy felt, at first, for the loss of his friend, those emotions of grief, which, on such occasions, enter into all men whose hearts are not composed of flint, or their heads of as solid materials?" (86) Later, for the sake of contrast, Fowler recasts Fielding's sentence into a more readily identifiable aphorism. The aim of this exercise is to reveal how otherwise "dogmatic surface structures" can be disguised and yet "still be cunningly asserted." Consider, now, Fowler's rewritten version: "Emotions of grief enter into all men whose hearts are not composed of flint or whose heads are not composed of as solid material" (87). Dealing with such heavily "disguised" aphorisms – that is, aphorisms almost unrecognizably "embedded into the narrative" (Gray, 270) – goes beyond the scope of the present study. Given that we are dealing with a largely untouched field of research, namely aphoristic phenomena within twentieth-century narrative prose in French, it seems advisable to limit the scope of study to the "very recognizable" form of aphorism and to leave more heavily "disguised" aphoristic discourse for a separate project.

In a recent publication, *Kafka's Aphorism: Literary Tradition and Literary Transformation*, Richard Gray needs seek no alternative to the term *aphorism* to conduct a discussion on Kafka's well-known collection of "Aphorismen," published posthumously in 1946. Aside from Kafka's creation of aphorisms per se, Gray sets out to demonstrate the author's "inclination toward aphoristic utterances" within the whole of the author's literary production (124). Indeed, Gray's leap from "aphorism" as the term was used by the writer he is studying to the more general concept of "aphoristics" (134) in the context of imaginative prose forms the pivotal substance of his research and implicitly posits the notion of the aphoristic writer of fiction: "My thesis will be that the periods of intense occupation with the aphorism represent the breakthrough of a tendency that had been perennially present, if latent, in Kafka's creative personality, and that it would remain a creative undercurrent throughout his life" (124). Gray's work is particularly useful, not only for its provocative ideas on "the marriage of aphoristic and novelistic form" (3) but also for the way it attempts to elaborate a history of both French and German aphorism.

Perhaps the single most thorough, concise, and well- organized treatise on the topic at hand is Harald Fricke's *Aphorismus*. Although the bulk of his research concerns "Klassiker des Aphorismus in deutscher Sprache" (70) and collections of aphorisms conceived as such by their authors, Fricke, too, goes on to elaborate something of a history of French aphorism. To a limited extent he also explores the role of aphorism within novelistic discourse, but in doing so he raises many more questions than he answers.

The strength of his method lies in the fact that only after he has observed the behaviour of aphorism in many contexts does he attempt to enumerate the specific elements and techniques that might constitute a distinct literary genre called *aphorism*. As it moves forward, Fricke's work not only traces the diachronic movement of French and German aphorism but also serves to modify and inform our present notions about it. Thus his research probably represents the most thorough and balanced attempt thus far to elaborate a comprehensive theory of aphorism and to define the genre.

Fricke cautions those embarking on any examination of aphorism against three common methods that, in his view, lead to erroneous results. First, there are those studies that

focus on a favorite author and/or a favourite type of aphorism and extrapolate their findings into a sweeping delineation of the genre. (4)

At the other end of the spectrum are authors who often limit themselves to a simple typology of aphoristic phenomena and completely sidestep the task of determining those characteristics common to the genre. (4)

A third deficiency lies in the widespread attempt to find, solely within an individual aphorism itself, sufficient criteria [to determine] whether it belongs to the genre. (3–4, translations mine)

Fricke particularly opposes the third approach and, taking one of Goethe's aphorisms ("Wer das erste Knopfloch verfehlt, kommt mit dem Zuknöpfen nicht zu Rande" "All the buttoning in the world won't help if you get the first button wrong.") as an example, sets out to convince his reader that "the wording of an isolated remark in no way suffices as a basis for classifying it as an aphorism; rather, text, co-text, and context must be considered together in order to establish that it belongs to the genre aphorism" (4, translation mine).

To arrive at a practicable definition of aphorism for his own work, Fricke traverses a morass of research carried out by other scholars. Two of these merit our brief attention.

Fricke refers somewhat exuberantly to Franz Mautner, author of *Der Aphorismus als literarische Gattung*, as "the father of aphorism research within the field of literary science." Mautner recognizes that aphoristic sentences occur not only as an independent genre but also as elements within the novel and the drama. He initially defines such sentences as "any otherwise undefinable, shorter prose utterance" (5). Fricke, however, seizes upon Mautner's later, more precise definition to inform his own study:

die 1) knappe sprachliche 2) Verkörperung eines 3) persönlichen 4) äusserlich isolierten 5) Gedankens [the 1) concisely formulated 2) embodiment of 3) a personal, 4) outwardly isolated 5) thought]. (5, translation mine)

Additionally, Fricke cites the research of R.H. Stephenson for articulating a crucial dilemma. Here, as is frequently the case, Fricke fluidly shifts his focus from the structural to the epistemological behaviour of aphorism. Stephenson brands as a cliché the idea that aphorism "conveys an unconventional, 'system'-contradicting thought." In his estimation an aphorism performs, rather, the exact opposite function, which is to express "'old hat' [*Altbekanntheit*], yes, even banality, through the subtle and artful employment of rhetorical devices" (6). This conflict – aphorism either as conveyor of "old hat" or of new, heretofore unthought-of ideas – represents still another issue to be borne in mind as we delve into the function of aphorism within contemporary francophone novels.

To gain insight into the vast array of influences acting together to shape Fricke's definition of the genre, we must read his study in full. A systematic explication of the definition might, however, compensate partially for the absence here of his contributive intertext. First, let us view the definition itself: "Ein Aphorismus ist ein kotextuell isoliertes Element einer Kette von schriftlichen Sachprosatexten, das in einem verweisungsfähigen Einzelsatz bzw. konziser Weise formuliert oder auch sprachlich bzw. sachlich pointiert ist." (An aphorism is a co-textually isolated element of a chain of written, non-fictional, semantically versatile prose texts, cast into a single sentence or into a concise form and containing a mordant reference, or provocative by reason of its content or its linguistic constitution (18, translation mine). The problems created by examining Fricke's definition in isolation from its own co-text are compounded by translating the sentence. This must be said so that the resulting transformation into English will not cast unfair doubt on Fricke's laudable endeavour both to clarify and consolidate and to expand the definitions of his predecessors.

On the question of how aphorism is used in novelistic discourse, Fricke's project must be seen only as an attempt to establish aphorism as an independent literary genre, alongside, say, poetry. For this reason he concentrates almost exclusively on collections ("chains") of aphorisms originally conceived as such by their authors. While Fricke admits that textbook examples of aphorism can appear in the novel (see the section on Jean Paul), he considers such manifestations of the genre to be so fraught with additional questions that he elects to dodge the issue (84).

Nevertheless, Fricke's move to define the genre proves worthwhile, for it succeeds in distinguishing aphorism from its sister genres. Further, the fundamentals he establishes act as convenient springboards into the realm of novelistic discourse.

With regard to Fricke's definition, it may be stating the obvious to say that such a compact, carefully thought-out genre as aphorism belongs mainly to the realm of written discourse. In an article on written language and imaginative fiction Margaret Rader, a linguist at the University of California Berkeley, enlivens an otherwise dry and all-too-obvious assertion. She challenges the widely prevalent view that writing is little more than grammatically and lexically complex language (195), that it is "decontextualized or autonomous language" (197), or worse yet that it preserves "the precise and explicit speech of the analytic philosopher, the scientist, and the bureaucrat" (186). In Rader's view, as opposed to Bennington's, writing need not necessarily inscribe "sententiousness" or "lay down the law." Instead, she contends, "Nothing intrinsic in the medium of writing dictates that no contribution should come from the reader." Indeed, Rader sets out to rehabilitate the written word, affirming that literary discourse by definition "make[s] possible the development of a complex image in the mind of the reader." Writing that achieves this end, she goes on to argue, "deserves to be placed along side of ... scientific prose as one of the ways gifted language users have explored the potential of language in its written form during the last two hundred years of Western culture" (187).

In this same vein, the argument Fricke puts forward on the non-fictional, exploratory character of aphorism might seem pedantically self-evident. By addressing the issue, however, he is able to separate aphoristic propositions from epigrams – the latter of which are often put into verse – and from aphoristic but fictional anecdotes and jokes (20). When we consider aphoristic sentences within the novel – by definition an imaginative genre – the question of an aphorism's non-fictionality becomes more complex. In isolation such aphorisms behave essayistically, or "objectively" (*sachlich*) – i.e., they focus clearly on some object or phenomenon in the extratextual world. However, as a functional element within their original (novelistic) habitat, they also complement the rest of the novel's more imaginative elements. How aphorisms behave within a given novel, and their possible value in isolation from it, are two of the key issues addressed throughout this study.

With regard to the assumption that aphorism is prose, Fricke simply opposes the genre in its purest, most condensed form to aphoristic poetry, dialogue, drama, and sketches (13–14, 20–1). One area of Fricke's definition serves, in its extreme compactness, to initiate a productive discussion: the question of the adjective *verweisungsfähig*. On the one hand Fricke seems to have chosen this derivative from the verb *verweisen* (among a host of other meanings, "to refer") to indicate that an aphorism acts as a signifier – that it fulfils a referential function. On the other, however, he insists that its "semantic reference is not immovably fixed" (15).

Jakob and Wilhelm Grimm's thoroughgoing *Deutsches Wörterbuch* analyses over several pages various incidences of *verweisen* and its derivatives with illustrations from prominent German texts. Two of their findings prove particularly enlightening when applied to Fricke's use of the word:

e) die verweisung [*sic*] enthält eine aufforderung. [a *verweisung* (the nominative form of *verweisen*) contains an invitation to do something].

a) auf ein ziel, eine aufgabe, eine verhaltungsweise oder einen gegegenstand v[erweisen], mit dem man sich beschäftigen soll [to point out a goal one should pursue, a duty one should carry out, a behaviour one should cultivate]. (2190, translations mine)

Fricke is sensible, however, throughout his study to avoid suggesting that an aphorism possesses only one definite referent – that it "lays down the law" on behalf of the author or even the text; rather, the diverse experiences that readers themselves bring to making sense of the aphorism is of overriding importance (140).

One might add, as a foreshadowing of the present study's more detailed look at the issue of referentiality, that an additional factor in the deferral of an aphorism's meaning will stem from the influence exerted by its co-text, in this case the novel. For example, a postmodern novel, built out of unconventionally compiled segments, might provide a greater number of possibilities than more traditional novels for attributing meaning to its aphorisms.

As is the case with most studies on aphorism, Fricke's work addresses the issue of length (for him *ein Einzelsatz*) as a determinant of the genre. While many of the various definitions embrace this "single-sentence" criterion, they also concede that it is mainly concision that indicates whether an utterance is an aphorism or not. Thus, in the final analysis, compactness overrides the notion of one sentence in determining whether a discourse unit is an aphorism.

Still another criterion common to most definitions of aphorism – the one of perhaps greatest import – is the idea that it must in some way provoke to thought or action. Fricke neologizes from the French to form the German adjective *pointiert* to convey, as economically as possible, the provocative qualities of aphorism. His lexical choice seems appropriate, for the adjectival derivative of the French noun *pointe* carries with it a rich semantic load, ranging from "evocative," "provocative," "pointed," "stinging," and "spiked" all the way to "barbed." The provocative features of an aphorism arise, according to Fricke, either from its rhetorical constitution or from the way it enters into a signifier/signified partnership with an "object." Again, it bears repeating that Fricke emphasizes repeatedly his view that as an aphorism takes on a signifying function, much depends on "active reception" and on the reader's particular field of knowledge and experience (140).

To round off this section on the definition and nature of aphorism, we may do well to listen to the (counter-) arguments of an unabashed anthologizer. John Gross has compiled a large quantity of texts in a recent publication, *The Oxford Book of Aphorisms*. In its brevity his three and one-half-page introduction, where he elaborates a method and a rationale, could have been guided by two of the sixteen aphorisms that inaugurate the collection:

Summaries that contain most things are always shortest themselves.

Samuel Butler, *Prose Observations*, 1660–80 (1)

It is my ambition to say in ten sentences what other men say in whole books – what other men do not say in whole books.

Nietzsche, *Twilight of the Idols*, 1888 (1)

It is evident from his bibliography that Gross has assimilated a substantial body of knowledge on aphorism. He has himself paid the price of first becoming "lost in [the] wilderness of definitions" (viii). Yet all this preparation carried out behind the scenes is only barely apparent in the anthology's introductory material. With a remarkable economy of words Gross reasons rapidly through to a few key conclusions. It therefore seems excusable, in the effort to define what an aphorism is and is not, to reproduce a lengthy excerpt from his introduction:

[Samuel] Johnson himself defined an aphorism, in what was by then its current sense, as a maxim; a precept contracted in a short sentence; an unconnected position. A maxim is also one of the definitions in the OED (along with a short pithy statement containing a truth of general import); ... Yet although the two words certainly overlap, they are far from interchangeable. An *Oxford Book of Maxims* would not, I think, sound particularly inviting: all too often a maxim suggests a tag, a stock response, something waiting to be trotted out in the spirit of Polonius. Aphorisms tend to be distinctly more subversive; indeed, it is often a maxim that they set out to subvert. And they are less cut and dried, more speculative and glancing ...

Without losing ourselves in a wilderness of definitions, we can all agree that the most obvious characteristic of an aphorism, apart from its brevity, is that it is a generalization. It offers a comment on some recurrent aspect of life, couched in terms which are meant to be permanently and universally applicable. But the same could be said of proverbs; and aphorisms, unlike proverbs, have authors. The third distinguishing mark of the aphorism, in fact, is that it is a form of literature, and often a highly idiosyncratic or self-conscious form at that. It bears the stamp and style of the mind which created it; its message is universal, but scarcely impersonal; it may embody a twist of thought strong enough to retain its force in translation but it also depends for its full effect on verbal artistry, on a subtlety or concentrated perfection of phrasing which can sometimes approach poetry in its intensity. (At the same time one should add that compression is not necessarily the supreme stylistic virtue in an aphorism, and that the finest examples are not always the most terse. A good aphorism – and here too it differs from a proverb, which has to slip off the tongue – may well need to expand beyond the confines of a single sentence.)   (viii)

Several of Gross's ideas call for a contrastive analysis with those of Fricke. Fricke agrees with Gross on the notion of the aphorism's "unconnected position," but only in the case of aphorisms that appear in "chains" or in collections originally designed as such by their authors. For Fricke the *Herausoperieren* (surgical removal) of aphorisms from an essay or a novel represents an evil to be avoided, and the resulting (bastardized) anthologies must be approached with "the greatest caution" (10). By contrast, Gross argues that an aphorism must simply be capable of standing alone.

This more all-encompassing premise then governs the whole of Gross's anthology project. His introduction also situates aphorism within "the wilderness of definitions" more succinctly than any more lengthy study, including Fricke's. However, with regard to proverbs, Fricke usefully adds to Gross's discussion by remarking that an aphorism may in time become a proverb, or a "common saying" (23). (In all other ways Fricke treats an aphorism and a proverb as nearly identical genres.) Gross's introduction also posits more forthrightly than Fricke – or any other study – the function of aphorism as "commenting on a recurrent aspect of life." Later we will see how Kenneth Burke elaborates on this assumption. For Burke the concise "naming of situations" (260) typically accomplished by proverbs constitutes the very substance of literariness.

Finally, whereas Fricke wants to confine aphorism to a single sentence, Gross does not hesitate to select longer texts for his anthology.

Gross's justification for doing so is humorous and trenchant, namely to avoid in his book "a rat-tat-tat of 'one liners'" (ix).

Before attempting to bring together all the salient elements from the preceding "wilderness" into a practicable delineation of aphorism, we might do well first to view a textbook example of the genre. This aphorism neatly demonstrates the various problems and issues explored thus far. Gross excerpts it from Virginia Woolf's *A Room of One's Own*: "Life for both sexes is arduous, difficult, a perpetual struggle. It calls for gigantic strength. More than anything, perhaps, creatures of illusion as we are, it calls for confidence in oneself. Without self-confidence we are babes in the cradle. And how can we generate this imponderable quality, which is yet so invaluable, most quickly? By thinking that other people are inferior to oneself" (72).

Besides having to reflect on the many factors that might constitute an aphorism *per se*, we must also bear in mind that the preceding example was taken from a larger context and that the elements that normally surround it could cause it to behave quite differently from the way it does as part of the "Self-Doubt" section of Gross's anthology.

For the purposes of this study the term "aphorism" seems the most apt of all possible shorthand symbols to conduct a coherent discussion of provocative "sententious" passages within francophone novels written during this century. None the less, we must realize that we are not employing an innocent, a *degré zéro* (Barthes) term; rather, we are consciously resorting to a ready-made signifier charged with complex baggage from the Western literary tradition. Thus, we may do well constantly to bear in mind that in choosing this term over another, we confine the whole phenomenon of aphoristics within the modern francophone novel into an *a priori* epistemological system.

Further, we can safely posit that, as part of that "system," aphoristic discourse is usually cast in the "timeless" present tense. The use of the present tense in the novel has the particular function of interrupting the narrative flow and calling attention to itself. For a moment there is a suspension of the recounting of particular events and descriptions, and a shift to the "generic" is effected.

An aphorism thus has general, or "generic" import. This import might be seen to arise from the way it conveys a revolutionary or, on the contrary, a banal or commonplace idea.

Aphorisms are concise and are frequently but not always confined to a single sentence. They are thought- and image-provoking, to the point of being caustic and subversive in their more extreme incidences. In their "strong" form, at least according to Fricke, they are found in "chains" that have been conceived, laid out, and published as such by their authors. However, the very genre that Fricke so painstakingly defines can be just as frequently observed as a part of narrative prose.

Although an aphorism that was originally placed into novelistic discourse is capable of making sense standing entirely alone, it will probably behave differently from the way it does when it performs within its larger context. This is to say that the function of aphorism varies, depending on whether it is part of an original "chain," a contrived anthology, a narrative, or is deployed independently – for example, as an epigraph.

Aphorism differs from its neighboring genres, but sometimes only slightly. Proverbs and aphorisms, for example, turn out to be very closely related; perhaps an aphorism differs from a proverb only in that the latter has forged its way into common speech because of the ease with which it "rolls off the tongue."

Aphorisms can fulfil a referential function, and yet their image-creating, thought-provoking nature implies an active, ofttimes volatile text/text-recipient relationship.

Fricke and Mautner have successfully argued that aphorism is a literary genre unto itself, although they take the matter still further and attempt to segregate it and then confer upon it a supposed purity. Who, however, is to forbid an aphorism from intermarrying – with the novel, for example – and thereby to create new permutations of textual function and signification?

THE NARRATOLOGICAL CONSEQUENCE OF APHORISM

The research of two eminent American linguists, William Labov and Paul Hopper, although not directly concerned with the study of literature, casts considerable light on a number of key narratological functions within novelistic discourse.

In 1972 the socio-linguist William Labov published the results of an exhaustive study of "Black English vernacular" (BEV) in his collection *Language and the Inner City*. One of the essays from that volume, "The Transformation of Experience in Narrative Syntax," is useful to a discussion of aphorism as it appears within the novel. Labov draws a number of challenging conclusions about narrative, having analysed vast quantities of recorded "casual inner-city" speech. In presenting his findings, he advances a few spare hypotheses, all supported by copious examples from the tapes he collected.

Nowhere did Labov make literary texts the object of study. However, he suggested that his discoveries could apply to a wide range of narratives (359). This conclusion provides an internal justification for extending his work to novels written in other languages.

Citing the samples he collected, Labov demonstrates that a "fully formed narrative" often displays six major sections:

1 Abstract
2 Orientation
3 Complicating Action
4 Evaluation
5 Result or Resolution
6 Coda   (363)

Labov tends to lump narrative "beginnings, middles and ends" into one general category, which he most often refers to as the "chain of actions" (366). He rightly observes that these "have [already] been analyzed in many accounts of folklore or narrative" (366). Such fundamentals of narrative therefore require no further commentary here.

To the remaining portion of the narrative structure, more germane to the purposes of this study, Labov assigns the name *evaluation*. Labov takes more interest in the evaluated part of the narrative than in the mere recounting of events. He defines evaluation as "the means used by the narrator to indicate the point of the narrative, its raison d'être: why it was told, and what the narrator is getting at. There are many ways to tell the same story, to make very different points, or to make no point at all. Pointless stories are met (in English) with the withering rejoinder, 'So what?'" (366). Having quickly identified the characteristics of the *récit* proper, or the unadorned chain of events, Labov then contrasts these readily identifiable elements with the more sophisticated set of elements that he feels make up the "evaluation" of that chain.

Labov argues that in English-language narratives the chief grammatical indicators of the simple story-line are "preterit verbs, simple past tense marker[s] and some past progressive" (376). He then ventures a more enterprising hypothesis in the further assertion that "evaluation" is "perhaps the most important element in addition to the basic narrative clause" (366). According to Labov, "evaluative" clauses can also be marked grammatically, just as the purely "narrative" ones are. He observes that, when functioning in evaluative clauses, verbs switch from the preterit or the imperfect (or sometimes the narrative present) of the indicative to other tenses and modes

(381). It is worthwhile to recall that Fowler too noted how the verbs in aphorisms suddenly break from the usual past tenses and instead are cast in the timeless, generalizing present tense.

Although Labov does not report any incidence of aphorism, or even sententious discourse, from his recordings and analyses of BEV, he establishes a very broad heading under which they might fit. He sets out to demonstrate that a narrator, when explicitly evaluating the chain of events he or she is reporting, "can stop the narrative, turn to the listener, and tell him what the point is" (371). Labov cites the blatant example of a certain narrator who frequently interrupted her story with such platitudinous evaluative remarks as "but it was quite an experience" (371).

An aphorism might be seen to produce an analogous effect – that is, of stopping the narrative flow and suggesting the point of the story. An aphorism, however, "tells the point" with far greater sophistication, wit, and subtlety than did the intervention of the aforementioned narrator. Additionally, the insertion within a *récit* of an aphorism whose verb suddenly switches to the timeless present tense has the effect of universalizing an otherwise specifically located story, and perhaps of causing an anonymous reader to liken it to personal experience.

As an example, let us consider Proust, who perhaps more frequently than any author from any period intercalates essayistic/aphoristic passages into his narrative. In the excerpt that follows he states the "point" of his enterprise in *A la recherche du temps perdu*: "D'ailleurs, que nous occupions une place sans cesse accrue dans le Temps, tout le monde le sent, et cette universalité ne pouvait que me réjouir puisque c'est la vérité, la vérité soupçonnée par chacun, que je devais chercher à élucider" (*Le Temps retrouvé*, 439).

It is reasonable to assume that aphoristic, generalizing formulations, with their abrupt switch into the present tense, form the technique par excellence by which Proust tells his reader the reason he is telling the story. Antoine Compagnon, in his introduction to the Folio edition of *A la recherche* complements this view with the assertion that the narrative voices in Proust's novel epitomize a fusion of "le héros passé et le narrateur présent" (*Swann*, vviii). As such, Proust's deployment of aphorism is one of the chief means whereby he seeks to elucidate, more powerfully than with a bare story-line, some "truth" he supposes to be "suspected by everyone." This underlying justification for aphorism in Proust's writing is significant, for it can reasonably be applied to other authors' work.

One might criticize Labov for a certain tendency towards totalization as he elaborates a perhaps too-neat taxonomy of narrative. As a counterfoil, Ludwig Wittgenstein's more plastic view of language is worth considering. In the *Philosophical Investigations* Wittgenstein offers a model of language whose main components are "language games" (39e, 83), fluid "propositions," or "signposts" (39e–40e) – three interrelated terms. For Wittgenstein a language-event can be likened to an overall game, itself composed of subgames (propositions or signposts). During the course of these "games" the rules are made up – or even altered as one goes along (39). Within a written narrative one might imagine the subgame "aphorism" bearing the title "NB: This is why I think this story is worth telling."

Had Ollendorff, to whom Proust initially submitted the manuscript of *A la recherche*, paid closer attention to the aphoristic "signposts" in the first thirty pages, he might been less baffled by the apparently banal story-line about sleeplessness and been prompted to share, as Grasset more shrewdly did, in the success of this seminal twentieth-century novel. Instead, Ollendorff summarily dismissed both Proust and his manuscript in these terms: "Je suis peut-être bouché à l'émeri, mais je ne puis comprendre qu'un monsieur puisse employer trente pages à décrire comment il se tourne et se retourne dans le lit avant de trouver le sommeil" (*Swann*, XXXII).

Taken in conjunction with one another, Labov's quasi-empirical and Wittgenstein's reflective-philosophical approaches begin to reveal the workings of aphorism as a lingual operation – in the particular case of novelistic discourse as a subfunction that occurs within the overall narrative structure.

The influential work of Paul Hopper on aspect, foregrounding, and backgrounding in discourse provides a valuable addition to Labov's research and takes us a step further in the exploration of aphorism as it functions in a narrative. In opening his study, Hopper independently corroborates Labov's parallel hypotheses on "narration" and "evaluation." Hopper, however, bases his conclusions on a nineteenth-century traveller's tale in Swahili and concludes that a fundamental difference exists between the sentences in the foreground (what he terms the "main line" events) and the sentences in the background (the "shunted" material). For Hopper the chief difference between the two lies in the fact that "backgrounded events usually amplify or comment on the events of the main narrative" (214). He elaborates by saying that "backgrounded clauses do not themselves narrate, but instead they support, amplify, or comment on the narration. In a narration, the author is asserting the occurrence of events. Commentary, however, does not constitute the assertion of events in the story line but makes statements which are contingent and dependent on the story-line events" (215–16).

Hopper then proceeds to enumerate the various features he believes to constitute backgrounded material. His findings prove especially useful in the case of narratives in French, for he embarks on a discussion of the *passé simple* (the French preterit), contending that it "is the foregrounding form of the verb in my framework" (217). Within Hopper's framework the *passé simple* favours, among other things,

- actions as opposed to states;
- affirmative as opposed to negative verbs;
- human subjects as opposed to non-human subjects; and
- singular subjects as opposed to plural subjects.

Also, the tense markers of the *passé simple* (i.e., "-ai," "-as," "-a," "-âmes," "âtes," "èrent") indicate in a concrete, observable way how verbs actually go about "favouring" the above situations (217).

In Hopper's schematics it follows that specialized verb morphology can likewise signal backgrounded clauses. Essentially, he contends that "backgrounding is indicated [in verbs] by a variety of formations that have in common the absence of the perfective-realis markers of foregrounding" (237). Hopper unfortunately leaves the present tense out of his discussion and focuses instead on markers of the imperfect, pluperfect, future, future perfect, and conditional as potential indicators of backgrounded clauses. He does, however, offer the incisive observation that verbs in foregrounded clauses – at least in the few languages he deals with – are usually "punctual, rather than durative or iterative" (215). The results of any switch within a narrative from the punctual (e.g., preterit) to the durative or iterative present are the same: in general, the latter serve to amplify or to comment on reported events. To be more exact, one could say that a verb's switch away from the punctual aspect tends to depict a "state or situation necessary for understanding motives" or simply to convey stasis of one kind or another, as opposed to re-presenting, via language, dynamic, kinetic events (216).

A problem in Hopper's method, at least for our purposes, arises from the fact that in French narratives the imperfect and the present, along with the *passé simple*, are often used to convey the actions of the story-line. In the case of the imperfect the events being recounted, instead of being completed action, either are habitual or were repeated an unspecified number of times. In the case of the "historical" or narrative present, this tense simply replaces the preterit to produce a more marked effect.

It may be helpful, after so many theoretical considerations, to look at three segments of actual novelistic discourse, so that the concepts of foregrounding, backgrounding, evaluation, and switching from one language-game to another (and therefore from one set of verb morphology to another) do not remain abstractions.

Gide's aphorism from *L'Immoraliste*, quoted at the outset, offers a textbook example of how a narrator inserts a pithy durative-iterative (or "timeless") sentence into a narration otherwise cast in the *passé simple*. "De nouveaux soins, de nouveaux soucis m'occupèrent; un savant italien me signala des documents nouveaux qu'il mit au jour et que j'étudiai longuement pour mon cours. Sentir ma première leçon mal comprise avait éperonné mon désir d'éclairer différemment et plus puissamment les suivantes; je fus par là porté à poser en doctrine ce que je n'avais fait d'abord que hasarder à titre d'ingénieuse hypothèse. *Combien d'affirmateurs doivent leur force à cette chance de n'avoir pas été compris à demi-mot!*" (166–7, emphasis added).

The second representative passage, also cited in part at the beginning of this study, is excerpted from the opening section of Proust's *A la Recherche* – from the very pages that caused Ollendorff to reject the novel. Throughout this section of the text Marcel, the narrator, recounts events from the past mainly in the imperfect, injecting all the while many essayistic and aphoristic reflections. The example that follows represents Proust's idiosyncratic conception of consciousness, the self, and otherness:

Sans doute le Swann que connurent à la même époque tant de clubmen était bien différent de celui que créait ma grand-tante, quand le soir, dans le petit jardin de Combray, après qu'avaient retenti les deux coups hésitants de la clochette, elle injectait et vivifiait de tout ce qu'elle savait sur la famille Swann, l'obscur et incertain personnage qui se détachait, suivi de ma grand-mère, sur un fond de ténèbres, et qu'on reconnaissait à la voix. *Mais même au point de vue des plus insignifiantes choses de la vie, nous ne sommes pas un tout matériellement constitué, identique pour tout le monde et dont chacun n'a qu'à aller prendre connaissance comme d'un cahier des charges ou d'un testament; notre personnalité sociale est une création de la pensée des autres. Même l'acte si simple que nous appelons "voir une personne que nous connaissons" est en partie un acte intellectuel.* (*Swann*, 18–19, emphasis added)

Finally, the following passage from Saint-Exupéry's *Terre des hommes* offers an example of how a narrative voice recounts past events using both the *passé-composé*/preterit and the present, then interposes an aphorism, it too cast in the present tense. In the case of the narrative proper, however, note how the aspect of the verbs is punctual. The verbs used to construct the aphorism are also in the present, but their aspect is durative-iterative. "J'ai atterri dans la douceur du soir. Punta Arenas! Je m'adosse contre une fontaine et regarde les jeunes filles. A deux pas de leur grâce, je sens mieux encore le mystère humain. *Dans un monde où la vie rejoint si bien la vie, où les fleurs dans le lit même du vent se mêlent aux fleurs, où le cygne connaît tous les cygnes, les hommes seuls bâtissent leur solitude*" (66–7, emphasis added).

Summing up thus far, it can be said that aphorism interrupts the flow of the main narration, that it temporarily suspends the "language-game" that simply reports events and constructs a story-line. The change in language-game boundaries is often marked by modifications in the morphology that indicates the verbs' tense and aspect. In the specific case of aphorism within French narratives the switch is from the *passé simple*, the imperfect, or the narrative present into the "timeless" present. An aphorism's purely narratological *raison d'être* is to amplify, to comment on, to universalize, and thus to elicit a more involved response to the story than if the aphorism were not present.

SOME EPISTEMOLOGICAL FUNCTIONS OF APHORISM IN NARRATIVE DISCOURSE

One might enunciate the essence of the task now at hand in the form of a question: When a reader is making sense of a text – specifically of a novel – what difference might the presence of an aphorism, or of aphorisms, make as the narrative unfolds? As we attempt to address in detail this "umbrella" issue, we confront what Humphries aptly viewed as "a conceptually treacherous terrain" (56). In order to maintain a degree of clarity as we venture through that terrain, it seems sensible to limit this rung of the discussion to two main topics: 1) What are some of the specific structural and referential behaviours of aphorism? 2) In the light of (1) above, how might an aphorism, or a novel's network of aphorisms, influence the way a reader receives a given literary text?

Harald Fricke enumerates the "Building Blocks for a System of Aphoristic Techniques" (140). We are in debt to Fricke, for in this concluding section of his book he relies entirely on his own research and presents comprehensive definitions not to be found elsewhere. His contribution in crystallizing a definition of the genre rests, there-fore, in the fact that he appears to be the first scholar to enumerate in any extensive way the many factors constitutive of aphorism.

Fricke begins by quoting from a study by Ulrich Greiner and then picks up where his colleague left off. Greiner had stated that "all the significant inquiries into the nature and form of aphorism account for the fact that an aphorism prompts an active [reader] reception. However, few if any explanations exist of how aphorisms actually go about performing this task, i.e., how they stimulate and cultivate such a reception" (140, translation mine). Fricke begins his own enumeration with these words of caution: "The procedures that are put forward are neither necessary nor adequate to determine whether a text is an aphorism or not (it is simply that, empirically, they occur frequently); and they are neither exhaustive nor disjunct – rather, they complement one another and overlap in many ways" (140, translation mine). The "procedures" Fricke refers to are grouped according to eight headings as follows:

1 Überspitzung (Exaggeration)

In Fricke's schematics *Überspitzung* serves as an umbrella heading under which a wide range of hyperbolic formulations might be classified. An author wittingly or unwittingly constructs the aphoristic text in such a way that it "goes recognizably too far" (140), with the effect that the reader is provoked to challenge the proposition in some way – into questioning it or into comparing it with personal experience. Some of the techniques used in the creation of such exaggerated propositions (translation of Fricke's examples are mine) might include:

Superlatives. As illustrated by "The costliest of all mistakes is a mistake of the heart" (141).

Antithesis. Here, two or more sharply contrasting polarities are brought together in a single statement – for example, "You can spurn the love of a woman in a number of ways: through trust and mistrust, through indulgence and tyranny, through too much and too little tenderness, through everything and through nothing" (141).

Sweeping Statements. According to Fricke, such formulations provoke a response as a result of being too plausible to be true. Often the desired effect is achieved by using the totalizing "never," "always," "all," "nothing," etc. Fricke offers a textbook example of this subgenre: "A man of spirit will not only never say anything stupid; he will never hear anything stupid" (142).

One must add, however, that *Überspitzung* in aphorisms, particularly many of those in the tradition of the French *moralistes*, may not have been designed to be questioned or to provoke contrary, speculative thought but rather to "lay down the law." Such aphoristic texts fall perhaps more into the realm of the maxim than into that of aphorism. Fricke refers to many such sentences as actual "allgemeine Verhaltensregel[n]" – that is, general rules of behaviour and not calls for critical thinking (142).

Finally, Fricke includes under the general heading of *Überspitzung* those aphorisms that contain some form of *definition*. These are short utterances that attempt to define or redefine a given notion. They can be taken seriously – that is, they make a sincere attempt to totalize – or they can bear discreet marks of irreverence, as in this specimen: "Remembrance – reminder of everything you didn't accomplish" (143).

2 *Aussparung (Understatement)*

In contrast to the foregoing, a further broad grouping is composed of aphorisms that create their effect by saying too little. Aphorisms of this type stimulate the reader's intellect by somehow compelling it to supply missing components. Divergences in the sense made of the aphorism will thus vary according to the unique baggage that the reading subject brings to the text.

This "completion" might be achieved through a wide range of devices, enumerated in part as follows:

Banality. Fricke cites a telling example: "There always falls a first snowflake, no matter what kind of tumult comes later" (145). Taken at its surface level, one might tend to rejoin with "So what?" However, if we go beyond the first level of signification, namely meteorology, the above *lieu commun* is transformed into an allusion to catastrophes and how they usually begin in seemingly insignificant ways.

Ellipsis. The example that Fricke offers to illustrate this aphoristic technique speaks for itself and requires no translation: "Kannibalismus – Militarismus – Nationalismus" (145).

Open-endedness. Incompleteness of a slightly different order than ellipsis is produced when the aphorism comes to an abrupt halt, and alludes to missing links in a possibly longer chain of signification: "A reader has it good: he can choose his authors" (146).

Concealed Meaning. In such incidences of aphorism the thought is enunciated fully; but on contemplating its perhaps obvious, or not-so-obvious secondary meaning, a caustic "pointe" is effected. Fricke cites this example: "Socialist brotherly love knows no bounds" (146).

3 *Überrumpelung (The Element of Surprise)*

The preceding techniques apply chiefly to the content, or to the referential qualities that may inhere in aphorisms. The next two main headings, by contrast, deal with some of those structural, lingual, or rhetorical devices that contribute to an aphorism's powers of evocation. The *Überrumpelung* section of Fricke's study proves slightly problematic within the present context, for most of the examples he has chosen work only in German. In other words, many of the salient features of an aphorism that he hopes will illustrate each subheading cannot be adequately translated into English. I have therefore in all but one case chosen analogous examples, written originally in English, taken from the *Oxford Book of Aphorisms*. The subheadings in question are 1) *neologism*, 2) various kinds of *word-play*, 3) a trenchant *rewriting of the familiar*, 4) *chiasmus*, and 5) *Schlusspointe* – a surprise twist of events to cap off an otherwise lacklustre thought (146–9). What follow are examples to illustrate, respectively, each of the above subheadings:

1 He would like to start from scratch. Where is *scratch?* (46, emphasis added)
2 Vision is the art of seeing things invisible. (238)
3 Style is nothing, but nothing is without its style. (310)
4 Who seeketh findeth not, but who seeketh not is found. (Fricke, 147)
5 While watching the ups and downs of reputations, I have often found myself exclaiming, 'Ah, the rats are leaving a *floating* ship.' (308, emphasis added)

Fricke somewhat erroneously views one additional characteristic of aphorism as being more structural than referential in nature, namely the capacity of an aphorism to *unmask* (*Entlarven*) an otherwise hidden truth. He therefore places this phenomenon under the rubric of *Überrumpelung*. From the single example he offers, however, it is far more difficult than in the other instances to ascertain where the aphorism's structural-lingual powers of evocation begin and its referential capacities leave off: "When hate turns cowardly, it goes masked into society and calls itself justice" (148).

4 *Verrätselung (Mystification)*

Here, certain lingual devices are fused to the concept of *Aussparung*, with the effect of provoking further thought from the reader. Perhaps the most primitive way to cause the reader to "complete" an affirmative proposition is to recast it so that it appears in the guise of a *question*: "Doth any man doubt, that if there were taken out of men's minds, vain opinions, flattering hopes, false valuations, imaginations as one would, and the like; but it would leave the minds of a number of men poor shrunken things, full of melancholy, and indisposition, and unpleasing to themselves?" (*Oxford*, 226)

For Fricke, the last four routes an aphorism might take to obscure its substance (and thus elicit a more active reader response) are the rhetorical devices of metaphor, simile, zeugma, and oxymoron. These tropes, however, are familiar enough to warrant no summary of his analysis here.

As a convenient example of an approach to another aspect of aphorism's signifying function, one that ties together everything said thus far, we might turn now to Richard Gray's work on Kafka. Gray attempts to link up historical context, author, authorial intent, and reader response. However, the work of the structuralists, the New Critics, and the French post-structuralists has taught us to problematize such an amalgam.

So, before we plunge too quickly into the thorny issue of authorial intent, the French thinker Paul Ricoeur offers a plausible intermediary approach. Throughout his career Ricoeur has retained the essence of his idiosyncratic hermeneutical model; however, he has not been afraid to modify it when revisions of traditional literary theories took hold (Thompson, 1–26).*

At the risk of oversimplifying a highly sophisticated and complex hermeneutical theory, we might take three of Ricoeur's central ideas – "distanciation," "the world of the text," and "appropriation" – to shed considerable light on aphoristic phenomena in the twentieth-century francophone novel. Ricoeur's conception of textuality and literariness constitutes an alternative but in some ways similar model to the more radical "indeterminacy" model ascribed to Derrida, de Man, and Lacan. It is then productive to fuse Ricoeur's three categories to Kenneth Burke's definition of literature as "proverbs writ large" (256). Proverbs, for Burke, articulate "typical, recurrent social situations" (255).

In Ricoeur's scheme of things, one of the fundamental aspects of textuality is the capacity to "project a world" (132). Before examining what this proposition means, we might do well to view from the outset what Ricoeur believes it does not. First, with the structuralists, he contends that the "world of the text" can "explode … the world

---

* Basic to the summary and discussion that follow are two articles included by John Thompson in his selection of Ricœur's essays, *Hermeneutics and the Human Sciences*, comp. and trans. John Thompson: "La Fonction herméneutique de la distanciation" and "Appropriation."

of the author" (139). Put more simply: "What the text signifies no longer coincides with what the author meant" (139). Neither does Ricoeur advocate a hermeneutical method based "on grasping an alien life which expresses itself through the objectification of writing" (140) – that is, on trying to grasp, for example, a novel's life and times. He goes so far as to assert that "this abolition of the ostensive character of reference is no doubt what makes possible the phenomenon we call 'literature'" (141).

Nevertheless, he sensibly qualifies this rationale, now practically become a received idea, with "there is no discourse so fictional that it does not connect up with reality" – no *degré zéro* of writing (141). These warring dialectics converge in a discerning question that reveals the nucleus of Ricoeur's thinking on the matter of textual "interpretation." He argues: "If we can no longer define hermeneutics in terms of the search for the psychological intentions of another person which are concealed behind the text, and if we do not want to reduce interpretation to the dismantling of structures, then what remains to be interpreted?" (141) In answer to the question he reiterates his conviction regarding an "abolition of a first-order reference" and further states that "this is the condition of possibility for the freeing of a second-order reference, which reaches the world not only at the level of manipulable objects, but at the level that Husserl designated by the expression *Lebenswelt* [life-world] and Heidegger by the expression 'being in the world'" (141).

The nexus between the reader's consciousness and the "second-order reference" to which Ricoeur refers is "the world of the text, the world proper to *this* unique text" (142). The reader's entry into and "interpretation" of this world can be achieved through two processes: "appropriation" and "distanciation."

Ricoeur borrows the word "appropriation" from the German *Aneignen*, which he defines as "'to make one's own' what was initially 'alien'" (185). This means that through the agency of a literary text, the reading "I" might be brought to "interpret – or to appropriate" all or part of "a proposed world which I could inhabit and wherein I could project one of my own most possibilities" (142).

Ricoeur takes pains to emphasize, however, that "appropriation is quite the contrary of contemporaneousness and congeniality: it is understanding in and through distance. It is not a question of imposing upon the text our finite capacity of understanding, but of exposing ourselves to the text and receiving from it an enlarged self" (143).

Ricoeur's phenomenological concept of appropriation also diverges from the widely popularized concepts of literature as a means towards self-recognition or self-identification – of seeing one's "good old" self enacted again and again in self-validating plots or characterizations. Rather, "appropriation" can only occur after the reading subject has achieved a certain "distanciation" – that is, through being shown "imaginative variations of the ego" (144). This "distanciation," for Ricoeur, "demands an internal critique," a "critique of the illusions of the subject, in a Marxist or Freudian manner" (140).

Ricoeur himself best summarizes the discussion thus far:

Far from saying that a subject, who already masters his own being-in-the-world, projects the *a priori* of his own understanding and interpolates this *a priori* in the text, I shall say that appropriation is the process by which the revelation of new modes of being – or if you prefer Wittgenstein to Heidegger, new "forms of life" – gives the subject new capacities for knowing himself. If the reference of a text is the projection of a world, then it is not in the first instance the reader who projects himself. The reader is rather broadened in his capacity to project himself by receiving a new mode of being from the text itself. Thus appropriation ceases to appear as a kind of possession, as a way of taking hold of ... It implies instead a moment of dispossession of the narcissistic ego.   (192)

Ricoeur of course nowhere addresses the question of aphorism in literature. None the less, his theory of textuality and literariness might elucidate the process by which aphorism contributes to "dispossession of the narcissistic ego" during the course of reading a novel.

To complete the grafting of Ricoeur's hermeneutics on to the concept of aphorism within the novel, however, we must first turn our attention to another conception of literature that complements Ricoeur's. In his classic essay "Literature as Equipment for Living" Kenneth Burke sets out to "violate current pieties, break down current categories and thereby 'outrage good taste'" (262). Burke inveighs against the traditional "inert" (262) (and therefore useless) literary typologies – for example, of the novel (261) – and instead pleads in favour of an innovative form of "sociological criticism" (253). This alternative mode of classification would be based on a series of "active categories" (262).

He sets up his line of argument with an analysis of proverbs. Burke contends that proverbs came into being in order to "size things up"; "to console and strike, to promise and admonish"; "to describe for purposes of forecasting" (259); for "vengeance" (254); and to illustrate "type situations" (253). In Burke's view "such naming was done not for the sheer glory of the thing but because of its bearing upon human welfare" (253).

He then makes a leap from the vernacular usage of proverbs to "the whole field of literature" (256). He asks rhetorically, "Could the most complex and sophisticated works of art legitimately be considered somewhat as 'proverbs writ large'" (256)? If we allow this premise to stand, literature then becomes (among many other things, certainly) a means for naming "typical, recurrent social situations" – or, in the terminology of Ricoeur: worlds. Moreover, the "names" in question are not developed out of "'disinterested curiosity,' but because [they] imply a command (what to expect, what to look out for)" (254).

This is not to imply, necessarily, that because a text "commands" it must be branded didactic. To illustrate the entire point at issue, Burke cites *Madame Bovary*, which, he argues, "singles out a pattern of experience that is sufficiently representative of our social structure, that recurs sufficiently often *mutatis mutandis*, for people to 'need a word for it' and to adopt an attitude towards it. Each work of art is the addition of a word to an informal dictionary" (259).

This comment constitutes another way of expressing the very idea that informs Richard Gray's thesis – that Kafka, because he explored and named modes of being and reality (but drew no conclusions), is an aphoristic writer (91–292), in spite of the fact that his novels exhibit few textbook examples of the genre itself. For Gray aphorism, to a greater extent than any other literary genre, induces "the hermeneutical interaction of the text and reader in which a progressive dialogue ensues upon the questioning of the reader by the text" (54).

Fricke can be seen to corroborate this radical claim by his definition of aphorism as a genre eminently capable of provoking the reader and causing the reader to reflect more actively (140).

To crystallize the foregoing discussion on the interpretive-strategic value of aphorism, it may be said that in novelistic discourse an aphorism can represent the point of juncture *par excellence* wherein a "fusion of horizons" (Ricoeur, 192) takes place. This notion of fusion might embrace the narrated chain of events, description, the experience of the author, and the experience of the reader.

A first step in identifying how an aphorism elicits a response from the reader is to analyse its purely structural characteristics. A mere structural analysis, however, that takes no account of an aphorism's potential to signify often results in a tedious impoverishment of the original text. One needs therefore to go beyond the bounds of formalism/structuralism in its strong form and propose that a novel's aphorisms, viewed both in their original narrative habitat and in anthologized isolation, allow particularly efficient access to what Ricoeur calls the "world of the text" and to what Kenneth Burke terms literature's inherent "equipment for living." John Gross offers a complementary thought when he argues that an aphorism – a terse, often poetic form – "bears the stamp and style of the mind which created it" (viii). It does not seem difficult to identify the relatedness inherent in the notions of stamp, style, mind, world, and equipment.

The move to include aphorism in the process of completing the hermeneutical circle or, by contrast, to access the "world of the text" is admittedly a blurry one. It would be misleading to use aphoristic weaponry in order to create new and definitive interpretations, or to determine once and for all the "first-order" – or any other – referents in a novel. Rather, through a heightened awareness of aphoristics in a given novel, a path might emerge, among many other possible ones, that can lead to an enhanced capacity on the part of the individual reader to make sense of a text and to access its world.

Aphorism also facilitates entry into Ricoeur's distanciation-appropriation dialectic, in that it can serve to make the reader more immediately aware of a heretofore ignored or neglected social situation. Recast in both Ricoeur's and Burke's language, aphorism, by virtue of its rhetorical and semantic constitution, may provoke a reader, more than will just the story-line itself, into "appropriating" a "proverb" and, by extension, an entire "equipment for living."

THE HERITAGE OF APHORISM IN
MODERN FRANCOPHONE LITERATURE

Whether there exists an idiosyncratically French "school" of aphoristic expression is an issue fundamental to this study. However, such a segregation of aphoristics into French, German, or any other national "model" turns out to be fraught with difficulties, as Richard Gray, whose work includes some contrastive analysis of German and French aphorism, is compelled to admit: "One is somewhat reluctant to relate these differences to national character or culture. In fact, the final intermingling of these separate types – or, perhaps more germane, the sublation of the dogmatic in the initiative aphorism – in the nineteenth and twentieth centuries goes against such cultural biases. Much more significant, of course, are temporal-historical considerations: the German aphorism evolves 150 years later than its French counterpart" (39). Thus, Gray must largely abandon the move to create French/German distinctions. Instead he suggests that conclusions be drawn based on the inherent features of aphorism and on "temporal-historical considerations."

A vast quantity of scholarly study has been carried out on the maxims, sentences, and aphorisms of the French *moralistes*. Most of these studies demonstrate how the pre-1800 French maxim tends to convey dogma, or "lay down the law." But the very term *moraliste* must be approached with caution. Heinz Krüger, in an investigation of aphorism entitled *Über den Aphorismus als philosophische Form*, challenges a notion prevalent outside of France: "The designation 'Moralist' provokes in the less delicate German usage quite the contrary to the French: 'moraliste' is neither the petty pedantic out to change the world nor the monumental purveyor of ethics out to present his ideas" (50, translation mine).

It seems more reasonable, and safer – even when discussing the French *moralistes* – to move away from a taxonomy of stereotypic national traits and to limit the discussion to features we know to have had currency in a specific country at a given time. To be sure, an impressive number of pre-1800 aphorisms in France might be deemed *Verhaltensregeln*, perhaps tried out first in the salons and then codified. And yet how many of the aphorisms coined by the best-known *moralistes* can be regarded as overtly didactic, heavy-handed, or univalent?

We may do well to consider for a moment some perhaps surprising examples of their work, not at all difficult to find in their collections, and ask to what extent scholarly effort to create sharp distinctions between the supposed "dogmatism" of the French moralists and the purported speculativeness of the German *Aphoristiker* prove fruitful.

Montaigne, considered to be the precursor of the seventeenth-century *moralistes*, offers this example of a relatively playful, speculative *réflexion morale*: "Il n'y a rien de mal en la vie pour celui qui a bien compris que la privation de la vie n'est pas mal" (37).

It was the "ascetic," ostensibly stolid Pascal who wrote this poly-valent example: "Les hommes sont si sincèrement fous, que ce serait être fou par un autre tour de folie, de n'être pas fou" (182).

The aphoristic *réflexions morales* of La Rochefoucault are characterized by their capacity to unmask human foibles through a minimum of direct preaching and a maximum of malicious play with words: "La vérité ne fait pas tant de bien dans le monde que ses apparences y font de mal" (65). It seems difficult to link this reflection with the word *moral* in its traditional sense.

Finally, a more provocative, open-ended La Bruyère than we might imagine: "Deux choses toutes contraires nous préviennent également, l'habitude et la nouveauté" (300).

It may reasonably be argued, as Gray actually does, that the French maxim of this period did tend to perform a "socially integrative function," whereas the development of aphorism in Germany over a century later was characterized more by a quasi-philosophical enunciation of *Einfall* – of "a sudden, unplanned, and unpredictable discovery of a unique insight" (44–5). Later, however, these two concepts overlap considerably in the aphorisms written in any country; and by the twentieth century the author of an aphorism is free to operate within an infinitely nuanced continuum, the opposite ends of which are speculativeness and dogmatism.

Indeed, as we explore French-language novels of the twentieth century, we will discern strong echoes of both traditions – of French moralim and of purportedly Germanic speculativeness.

To illustrate the latter "tradition," consider one of Nietzsche's aphorisms: "Der Glaube an die Wahrheit beginnt mit dem Zweifel an allen bis dahin geglaubten Wahrheiten." (Belief in the truth begins with calling into question all truths heretofore accepted as such. 1:750, translation mine.) The speculativeness of the proposition is effected by the repetition in modified form of the terms *truth/truths* and the dialectical presentation of belief/doubt.

It might reasonably be concluded, however, that the echoes of the French *moralistes* prove clearer and more persistent in the francophone corpus than in other bodies of literature.

THE EXTRACTION OF APHORISMS FROM NOVELISTIC DISCOURSE AND THEIR SUBSEQUENT ARRANGEMENT INTO AN ANTHOLOGY

Bennington, in part I, section 8 of his study, presents an incisive analysis of the uses and abuses of aphorism anthologies. In the case of the eighteenth-century novel, the practice of lifting aphorisms or maxims from the original text and then reformatting them has been widespread. Thus, ample material for analysis exists. From Bennington's observations, two main issues emerge that need to be addressed in this context: first, which aphoristic formulations are "liftable," and second, how they should be arranged once they have been isolated from the text.

When one encounters, within a narration, a fully formed aphorism cast in the present tense, the task of extraction presents no difficulty. Often, however, as we observed with *Tom Jones*, the author of a novel more or less imperceptibly weaves an aphoristic reflection into the fabric of the narrative. This means that a disguised aphorism can be included as a component of reported speech, can be ascribed to the reflexive consciousness of one of the characters, or can be part of a more lengthy, more overt passage of essayistic "intervention." When this kind of "embedding" of aphorisms occurs, the author must often cause the tense of the verb(s) to agree with the surrounding tenses rather than cast them into the "timeless" present, or an otherwise textbook aphorism may simply begin with an indicator of indirect discourse, such as "she said" or "he thought." In such cases an anthologizer must make an arbitrary decision on where to draw the line. Does one lift only the "pure" specimen, or does one slightly rewrite an aphoristic sentence so that it can act more independently?

With regard to the "rewriting" option, Bennington selects Bette Silverblatt's study of Duclos's *Les Confessions du comte de **** as a representative example and demonstrates how, through minimal rewriting, she could have listed not 109 sententious propositions from the novel but 179 (61).

The present study will limit itself largely to examining fully formed, clear-cut aphorisms. Two exceptions will be made, however, in the instances of Gabrielle Roy's *Alexandre Chenevert* and Claude Simon's *La Route des Flandres*. The rationale for going beyond fully formed aphoristic sentences will be explained in the relevant chapters.

Why lift aphorisms from a novel at all? Bennington speculates that one's chief motivation for taking such a course, at least in the domain of the eighteenth-century novel, has been (and he quotes Derrida) to "monumentalize inscriptions now made lapidary: 'the rest' in peace" (57). In other words, the anthologizer sets out to rescue the essence, the "surplus" of a novelistic text and to create a monument to it. In this connection Bennington appropriates a notion from Freudian psychoanalysis to make his point. He sees the drive to anthologize as a "manifestation of repressed anality; the precious metal of the maxim is easily enough identified with the faeces, a 'reste' detached from the body. The 'orderliness' of the anthology can also be linked to Freud's description of anal eroticism" (56). Bennington alludes here to the kind of anthology that seeks to extract sententious propositions from a novel and then to reclassify them into "eternal" rubrics: "Man," "Love," "Life," and the like.

The objectives of this study clearly diverge from those of such anthologizers. The main thrust here is not to "monumentalize" but to analyse the behaviour of aphorism within narrative. For this reason a separate listing of each novel's aphorisms is appended to the body of the text. The aphorisms, however, are arranged in the order they appear in the novel and not in a new-and-improved sequence bent on some extratextual criterion of "orderliness."

The opportunity to peruse a separate listing of a novel's aphorisms might prove beneficial for several reasons. First, such a format allows us to present and discuss evidence succinctly and clearly. Additionally, it may be helpful to be able to find and consult certain individual aphorisms at a glance and then refer back to the original context. It is also enlightening to review a given novel's aphorisms collectively. Through such a reading we obtain, for example, either an *a priori* or an *a posteriori* overview of the extent to which an author thinks and writes aphoristically. An overview of this kind can in turn help to reveal, in concise form, the "stamp and style" of an author and of his or her work.

Such an enumeration also provides one way to discern efficiently the topic chains, the essential substance of a text's "world." Particularly in the case of an "indecipherable" narrative such as Claude Simon's *La Route des Flandres*, a prior awareness of the novel's spare flashes of compressed *Denkökonomie* (Gray, 266) might form the basis of a pre-reading exercise or of a concentrated, specialized reading of the text. The uninitiated reader in particular could "scan" the text's (at first reading) disconnected narratological elements and make better sense of them after having become familiar with the philosophical/ subjective parts of the text.

However, even in the case of a less problematic text – for instance, Saint-Exupéry's blatantly sententious *Terre des hommes* – a look beforehand at some of the work's key aphorisms in a classroom setting can prepare the novice to appreciate the book's plotless, seemingly disjointed collection of *récits*.

We hardly need to be reminded that such "postmodern" narrative practices as these two have become increasingly common in literature produced during this century; spotting a work's aphorisms and focusing attention on them may facilitate the process of making sense of such difficult texts.

A brief word on how the foregoing theoretical considerations will relate to each of the seven novels is in order at this point. The texts that compose the cross-section for study are too diverse with regard to style and content to be submitted to a rigid mapping of the theory on to the novel. Therefore, as we proceed into the next stage, it seems more sensible simply to bear in mind the many ways in which aphorisms *may* function narratologically, and to consider how they might create meaning in a given context. From each novel inherent tendencies may thus emerge. While a given part of the theory might serve particularly well to elucidate a given tendency, it would be tendentious to force upon each text mechanically all the theoretical considerations elaborated thus far.

3 *Terre des hommes*

EXTRATEXTUAL CONSIDERATIONS

It is not surprising that Antoine de Saint-Exupéry would demonstrate a penchant for aphoristic discourse, in light of his early attraction to Nietzsche and his lifelong admiration for Pascal. Whether it is a question of influence or simple affinity matters little for our purposes here; suffice it to say that we are often reminded of the sententious-aphoristic style of these two predecessors as we read Saint-Exupéry's text. The most clear-cut manifestation of the style in question occurs in Saint-Exupéry's highly aphoristic *Citadelle*. Published after his death, the text in its formal structure effects something of a synthesis of Nietzsche's *Zarathustra* and Pascal's *Pensées*. The near absence of narration in the work is replaced by a curious litany of aphorisms, Pascalian in form and Nietzschean in substance.

Numerous passages within Saint-Exupéry's body of writings testify to his veneration of Pascal. This sentence from *Terre des hommes* might be taken as representative: "l'apparition d'un Pascal pauvre pèse plus lourd que la naissance de quelques anonymes prospères" (190). Saint-Exupéry also wrote that "pendant la guerre" (1939–44) "one of his most faithful companions was Pascal" and that "les œuvres de Pascal ... sont près de moi, sur ma table" (*Ecrits de guerre*, 164).

As regards Nietzsche, a brief, rather unobtrusive passage in *Courrier Sud* hints at Saint-Exupéry's youthful attachment to the German thinker and to his unconventional approach to life and art. In the novel Saint-Exupéry couches his own identity in the book's main character, Jacques Bernis, through whom he tells of a (figurative?) return to his boyhood home. Bernis/Saint-Exupéry there encounters several teachers from his former *collège*. This revisiting of childhood haunts has just followed a rigorous apprenticeship as a pilot, an event that corresponds conceivably to the author's own stint at Cap Juby.

Before making the point, however, it is instructive to insert Saint-Exupéry's autobiographical account of a decisive portion of his 1927 experience at that coastal outpost of northwest Africa: "J'emporte Nietzsche sous mon bras. J'aime ce type immensément. Et cette solitude. Je m'allongerai dans le sable à Cap Juby et je lirai Nietzsche. Il y a des choses que j'adore, mon cœur où se consume mon été, cet été court, chaud, mélancolique et bienheureux" (Estang, 38).

In *Courrier Sud* the narrator portrays his professors, particularly the one who taught philosophy, as formalistic, absolute. When Jacques Bernis has become an adult and his professors no longer have any reason to maintain their posture of dignified attitudinizing, the author-narrator speculates on how Nietzsche must have disquieted the former philosophy teacher. The teacher allows old inhibitions to fall, and at the time of their later encounter betrays a hint of regret for his antiquated, totalizing modes of teaching.

We must first take into account the fact that during Bernis's former school-days, this teacher (a transposition of one of Saint-Exupéry's professor's at the Jesuit *collège* at Le Mans?) had claimed "there was no more cruel enemy than Nietzsche for a graduate from secondary school." We then can appreciate how Jacques Bernis, with a hint of ironic triumph, thinks he detects not disdain but a trace of "tendresse coupable" on the part of the teacher for the German philosopher-essayist-critic (31).

The point of looking at this enigmatic sequence from *Courier Sud* is to demonstrate Saint-Exupéry's own "tendresse" for Nietzsche. Taking the point a step further, we note that the passage provides a valuable indication of the author's idiosyncratic brand of humanism. Luc Estang explains concisely: "Saint-Exupéry n'aura pas été troublé [as was the philosophy teacher]. Il sera allé dans Nietzsche – celui-ci meurt l'année même qui voit naître celui-là – comme 'on va toujours, en fin de compte vers où l'on pèse.' L'aura séduit, chez l'auteur de *La volonté de puissance* un style, cette qualité d'être à quoi il fut toujours attentif" (38). Estang later expands this fundamental assertion: "L'humanisme classique demandait: Qu'est-ce que l'homme? Un humanisme moderne, peu ou prou existentiel et de filiation nietzschéenne demande: Que peut l'homme? L'humanisme exupérien articulerait volontiers les deux interrogations l'une sur l'autre pour une sorte de synthèse, et demanderait: Que sera l'homme?" (107)

Saint-Exupéry and his humanist ethic have now fallen into some disrepute after the accolades during the years ranging, roughly, from 1940 to 1970. His view of civilization and humanity is none the less worth understanding, if only from a literary-historical standpoint. A focused look at the aphorisms in *Terre des hommes* will reveal much about the "humanisme exupérien" to which Estang refers. Moreover, the exercise might serve to demonstrate that Saint-Exupéry's thought is not as shallow as many critics have asserted.

For this study, why select *Terre des hommes* out of Saint-Exupéry's entire corpus? Although *Le Petit Prince* and *Vol de nuit* are more widely read, it may be reasonably argued that *Terre des hommes* represents his most polished work – André Gide thought so (Estang 78) – and that it provides the most concise overview possible of the humanist ethic in question. One of Saint-Exupéry's biographers, Georges Pélissier, would take issue, however, and argue in favor of *Citadelle*: "Et c'est cependant dans ce grand ouvrage qu'il faut chercher l'accomplissement de sa pensée et le couronnement de son œuvre" (88). The "cependant" alludes to another of Pélissier's perceptions, namely that *Citadelle* forms "a diffuse book" with a "superabundance of text" (88). Even if we were to accept Pélissier's argument, *Citadelle* proves unsuited for an analysis of the function of aphorism as an integral part of narrative, for the text contains only a few reported events, scattered disparately amid an admixture of poetry, essay, aphorism, and quasi-scriptural injunctions.

On the question of genre, although Saint-Exupéry chose to call *Terre des hommes* simply a *récit*, we might safely regard it as a novel. The *Académie* did when it awarded him the Grand Prix du Roman in 1939. Rather than being composed of a single *récit*, the book is made up of several *récits commentés*, which Pélissier deemed, aptly, *prétextes à la méditation* (68). Each account is supposed to be based on actual experiences from Saint-Exupéry's life, a thought that lends a certain immediacy to the narration. Perhaps of greatest value for the aims of the present study is the clean division in the book between the *récits* and the accompanying meditation/commentary: such an unproblematic narrative structure affords a convenient introduction to the more complex narratives to be featured later on.

A final extratextual issue fraught with potential difficulties needs to be confronted, namely Saint-Exupéry's own aversion to having his work "décompos[é] en éléments disparates" (Chevrier, 87). The question pertains not only to Saint-Exupéry's text but to all the other works treated in this study. Through the agency of metaphor Saint-

Exupéry in *Citadelle* inveighs against critical methods of "découpage et de reconstitution." Such a methodology, in his estimation, reduces "en tas de pierres ordonnées la cathédrale" (Chevrier 164). The issue is not whether one needs to remain bound to Saint-Exupéry's wish; rather his remark can be seen to initiate a propitious discussion on the merits of literary analyses that "cut and paste" and thereby run the risk of deforming the original text.

Since we will view a large quantity of individual aphorisms both in and out of their original context, my aim will be to glean as many insights as possible from the analytic process, but then to return to the text and consider any newly acquired knowledge in terms of the work as a whole. Also, in the separate lists of a given novel's aphorisms, the order in which they appear within the original text is respected; that is, no effort has been made to reclassify them according to an arbitrary set of text-external criteria.

THE NARRATOLOGICAL CONSEQUENCE OF APHORISM

In analysing the behaviour of aphorism in *Terre des hommes*, we encounter relatively few problems, for Saint-Exupéry tends not to disguise his aphorisms or to "embed" them deep in the narrative structure. This means that most of the work's aphoristic formulations are fully formed, integral entities and as such can be readily isolated and observed.

The most sensible way to proceed in the case of *Terre des hommes* is to look first at Saint-Exupéry's own introduction to the book and then to consider each of the eight chapters in succession.

The text's brief introductory remarks, set off from the rest of the novel, contain three aphorisms that might be regarded as a summation of the author's *Lebensphilosophie*, of his approach to literature generally, and of this text specifically. The first sentence of the entire work is a polemical statement in the form of an "overstated" aphorism: "La terre nous apprend plus long sur nous que tous les livres" (9). There follows its explanatory corollary: "L'homme se découvre quand il se mesure avec l'obstacle" (9). A short sequence ensues in which the author recounts, in the imperfect tense, a crucial part of his first night flight. In textbook fashion – if we adhere to Labovian schematics – a rather sententious aphorism (see "Il faut bien") caps off the narration and serves to enunciate the "point" of the entire story: "Il faut bien tenter de se rejoindre. Il faut bien essayer de communiquer avec quelques-uns de ces feux qui brûlent de loin en loin dans la campagne" (10).

The first chapter, entitled "La Ligne," announces the narrative structure (an alternation between reporting in the first person and essayistic commentary) of the entire work. As yet Saint-Exupéry does not mix genres; more specifically, this first *récit* flows, uninterrupted by extraneous commentary, for some twenty-two pages. A separate "essay-meditation" section then rounds off the chapter. This concluding section begins with an aphorism that, through the use of "Ainsi," links it to the preceding narration: "Ainsi, les nécessités qu'impose un métier, transforment et enrichissent le monde" (33). While the entire segment can be viewed as aphoristic, most of its sentences prove incapable of making sense on their own. The beginning sentence, however, is practically a full-blown aphorism, capable both of commenting on the surrounding narration and of assuming independence from it. One only need omit the first word, "Ainsi," to give it a life of its own.

The "anthology"-appendix for this novel, at the end of the study, presents a very few "embedded" aphorisms reworked to form freestanding texts. A discussion of the rationale for rewriting such sentences at all might prove useful at this introductory stage. First, consider this original text: "Dès lors, nous nous sentîmes perdus dans l'espace interplanétaire, parmi cent planètes inaccessibles, à la recherche de la seule planète véritable, de la nôtre, de celle qui, seule, contenait nos paysages familiers, nos maisons amies, nos tendresses" (28). The fundamental nature of the thought is so aphoristic and, in its pithiness, so essential to understanding the rest of the work that it ought to be included in the novel's "chain" of aphorisms. Additionally, only a minimum of rewriting is required, so the meaning of the original formulation remains intact: "[La terre:] la seule planète véritable, ... la nôtre, ... celle qui, seule, cont[ient] nos paysages familiers, nos maisons amies, nos tendresses" (28).

The preceeding aphorism demonstrates why many critics deem Saint-Exupéry to be shallow. Of course this earth is the only one we have to live on. However, if we consider the word *earth* metaphorically – that is, in the same sense as "down to earth" – the idea is no more shallow than the same line of reasoning in *Thus Spake Zarathustra*.

Throughout this study I have resorted to such rewriting of the original text rarely and advisedly. More often it has only been necessary to strip away any introductory "fillers" that relate the aphorism to its preceding narrative. Let us recall, for example, the simple omission of "Ainsi" so that the aphorism we just viewed on page 33 becomes capable of making sense on its own.

"Les Camarades" (chapter 2) begins with a short narrative lasting some five pages about the aviator Mermoz. An aphorism appears rather intrusively at the end of the story, arguably (cf. "Telle est la morale que") as a justification for recounting the experience: "Telle est la morale que Mermoz et d'autres nous ont enseignée. La grandeur d'un métier est, peut-être, avant tout, d'unir des hommes: il n'est qu'un luxe véritable, et c'est celui des relations humaines. En travaillant pour les seuls biens matériels, nous bâtissons nous-mêmes notre prison. Nous nous enfermons solitaires, avec notre monnaie de cendre qui ne procure rien qui vaille de vivre" (40). For the purposes of establishing as a separate entity this novel's "chain" of aphorisms, "Telle est la morale," a transitional device, is omitted.

Still in the second chapter of *Terre des hommes*, another sequence of reported events is presented to reinforce the first. This second segment of *récit* concerns another aviator, Guillaumet. It too is rounded off by an aphorism closely related in meaning to the first: "On s'élargit par la découverte d'autres consciences. On se regarde avec un grand sourire. On est semblable à ce prisonnier délivré qui s'émerveille de la mer" (43). The two aphorisms in the chapter thus comment on the preceding narration and are designed to convey the same "point" – that is, that the value of work and sacrifice must be measured mainly in terms of the human relationships that result from them.

We encounter five aphorisms in the next chapter, "L'Avion." The medley of topics introduced in this third chapter is directly reflected in the diversity of the thematic substance of the five aphorisms in question. The topics under discussion are the pitfalls of materialism, the inadequacy of language, and the possible value of technological advances. The fifth aphorism, speaking to the merit of the "tools" that humanity has created, serves to sum up the entire meditation: "Au delà de l'outil, et à travers lui, c'est la vieille nature que nous retrouvons, celle du jardinier, du navigateur, ou du poète" (61).

Chapter 3 dispenses entirely with reporting events and in so doing resembles more an essay than a narrative sequence from a novel. Its verbs are for the most part in the durative or iterative present and thus have the effect of universalizing the entire section. Passages of this kind, frequent in *Terre des hommes*, render problematic the task of delineating the boundaries between essayistic-aphoristic clusters of sentences and pure aphorisms. As a guideline for determining which of the sentences from the novel's "commentary" sections represent textbook cases of aphorism and which do not, I have relied largely on the notion of *Denkökonomie* and on the criteria established by Fricke.

The topic of chapter 4 is announced by its heading, "L'Avion et la Planète," and by its two initial sentences: "L'avion est un instrument sans doute, mais quel instrument d'analyse! Cet instrument nous a fait découvrir le vrai visage de la terre" (63). By now Saint-Exupéry is fluidly intermingling narration and aphorism, almost indiscriminately combining the fundamental story-line with "evaluation" of it (recalling Labov's terminology). In this chapter three aphorisms interrupt the narrative flow in order to comment on the reported events. When observed together they form a gradation, a provocative chain of ideas on the precarious nature of earthly existence:

Dans un monde où la vie rejoint si bien la vie, où les fleurs dans le lit même du vent se mêlent aux fleurs, où le cygne connaît tous les cygnes, les hommes seuls bâtissent leur solitude.   (67)

Dans quel mince décor se joue ce vaste jeu des haines, des amitiés, des joies humaines! D'où les hommes tirent-ils ce goût d'éternité, hasardés comme il sont sur une lave encore tiède, et déjà menacés par les sables futurs, menacés par les neiges? Leurs civilisations ne sont que fragiles dorures: un volcan les efface, une mer nouvelle, un vent de sable.   (68)

Nous habitons une planète errante.   (69)

Both the narration per se and the above "chain" culminate in the following aphorism, which brings the chapter to a close: "Ah! le merveilleux d'une maison n'est point qu'elle vous abrite ou vous réchauffe, ni qu'on en possède les murs. Mais bien qu'elle ait lentement déposé en nous ces provisions de douceur. Qu'elle forme, dans le fond du cœur, ce massif obscur dont naissent, comme des eaux de source, les songes ..." (78). "Maison" constitutes an archetypal metaphor that signifies various forms of "shelter" located outside the subject's seat of consciousness. For Saint-Exupéry, particularly in this text, the ultimate shelter, the ultimate "maison," is the earth itself.

The three chapters that follow, "Oasis," "Dans le désert," and "Au centre du désert," form a narratological trilogy practically devoid of aphorism. Nevertheless, the narrative voice frequently intervenes to "evaluate," but in alternative ways. These three chapters centre around the account of an actual experience in the desert in which the author and his flight companion, Prévot, nearly died of exhaustion and dehydration.

The two aphoristic passages that do appear within this, the narrative core of the novel, call for analysis. At one point the author-narrator thought he was "foutu" and contemplates, but only for a moment, the possibility of death. From this contemplation emerges an aphorism built around two disparate ideas: "L'idée qu'il mourra peut-être trente ans plus tard ne gâte pas les joies d'un homme. Trente ans, trois jours ... c'est une question de perspective. Mais il faut oublier certaines images" (160).

The two flight companions are finally rescued by a Bedouin who happens by and offers them water. The experience yields this aphoristic, lay-phenomenologist insight, reminiscent of the "chosisme" of Francis Ponge:

Eau, tu n'as ni goût, ni couleur, ni arome, on ne peut pas te définir, on te goûte, sans te connaître. Tu n'es pas nécessaire à la vie: tu es la vie. Tu nous pénètres d'un plaisir qui ne s'explique point par les sens. Avec toi rentrent en nous tous les pouvoirs auxquels nous avions renoncé. Par ta grâce, s'ouvrent en nous toutes les sources taries de notre cœur.

Tu es la plus grande richesse qui soit au monde, et tu es aussi la plus délicate, toi si pure au ventre de la terre. On peut mourir à deux pas d'un lac d'eau salée. On peut mourir malgré deux litres de rosée qui retiennent en suspens quelques sels. Tu n'acceptes point de mélange, tu ne supportes point d'altération, tu es une ombrageuse divinité.   (187)

These aphoristic passages are crucial not only to understanding the "point" of the story; they also bear upon the reader's ability to access the "world" of Saint-Exupéry's Exupérian text and to discern the "equipment for living" it proposes.

The final chapter of the novel consists mainly of an extended essay-meditation. It is enhanced, however, by four brief pieces of narration. In this instance, because of the ratio of narrative to commentary, it would appear that the narration complements the essay-aphorism portion of the text rather than the contrary. The chapter commences with a transitional allusion to the near-death experience just recounted in the previous chapter: "Je me suis cru perdu, j'ai cru toucher le fond du désespoir et, une fois le renoncement accepté, j'ai connu la paix. Il semble à ces heures-là que l'on se découvre soi-même et que l'on devienne son propre ami" (189). The narrator then generalizes the experience – that is, he paves the way to a more universally applicable discussion – with the question, "Comment favoriser cette sorte de délivrance?" The remainder of the book, which responds in some detail to this overall question, often relies on the economy of aphoristic discourse to enunciate a critique of contemporary Western civilization and to put forward a comprehensive, albeit highly idealistic, remedial plan.

The aphorisms in question are listed in Appendix A. An analysis of them, however, offers no additional insights into the narratological function they perform.

INSIGHTS GAINED FROM A SEPARATE LISTING OF THE NOVEL'S APHORISMS

Although Saint-Exupéry became preoccupied with Nietzsche early in life, little of the German philosopher's style – as opposed to the substance of his writing – manifests itself in the French author's corpus. Perhaps surprisingly, few of Saint-Exupéry's aphorisms bear Nietzschean stylistic hallmarks, namely the employment of playful, enigmatic, self-conscious rhetoric and the omnipresence of barbed "pointes." We may do well to consider one particularly terse sample as a reminder of Nietzsche's style: "Die Liebe vergibt dem Geliebten sogar die Begierde." (Love forgives the lover even for lust/passion/ desire. ii, 80:62, translation mine.) Compare the highly dynamic con- stitution of Nietzsche's reflections with the more straightforward style of the *moraliste* Pascal (whom Nietzsche said he disdained): "Qui voudra connaître à plein la vanité de l'homme n'a qu'à con- sidérer les causes et les effets de l'amour" (79–80:162).

Only rarely do Saint-Exupéry's aphorisms resemble those of Nietzsche, stylistically speaking – although the ideational content of the two frequently coincides. In *Terre des hommes* the only aphorisms that even come close to Nietzsche's style are the antithetical sentence fragment "Poussés par cette haine, ou cet amour" (112), or perhaps the only slightly enigmatic "La nostalgie, c'est le désir d'on ne sait quoi … Il existe, l'objet du désir, mais il n'est point de mots pour le dire" (201).

Occasionally Saint-Exupéry does infuse his aphorisms with para- nomasia, synechdoche, or with zeugmatic word-plays. Although they might contain such elements of rhetorical artifice, his aphorisms distinguish themselves from their Nietzschean counterparts by their altogether more sober and univalent tone.

To illustrate the point, contemplate one of Saint-Exupéry's apho- ristic sentences, constructed as a chiasmus: "Certes les *vocations* aident l'homme à se *délivrer*: Mais il est également nécessaire de *délivrer* les *vocations*" (192, emphasis added).

Thus, for the most part, aphoristics in Saint-Exupéry's text fall squarely into the tradition of the French moralists. His aphorisms tend to be – invoking Gray – "integrative" rather than "antagonistic" (43). While they are, to be sure, capable of stimulating further reflec- tion on the part of the reader, their effect is achieved through rela- tively straightforward semantic means.

Moreover, they are often designed to provoke the reader into some kind of concrete action in the extratextual world. By way of contrast, the Nietzschean or "antagonistic" variety of aphorism is often conceived so as to involve the reader in an exercise that is more cerebral than practical. To justify this contention, consider only two of many typical "integrative," largely unidimensional aphorisms found throughout *Terre des hommes*: "Mais nous n'avons pas besoin de la guerre pour trouver la chaleur des épaules voisines dans une course vers le même but" (209); and "Quand nous prendrons conscience de notre rôle, même le plus effacé, alors seulement nous serons heureux" (210).

If we bear in mind the various techniques that Fricke identified as potentially constitutive of the genre *aphorism*, the listing at the end of the study reveals a propensity on Saint-Exupéry's part to formulate hyperbolic, defining, and blatantly didactic aphorisms. Even a perfunctory perusal of the appendix will reveal how many of the aphorisms contain superlatives aided by such qualifiers as *avant tout, ne ... que, ne ... rien, ne ... point, plus rien, seul*, etc.

Before we leave the topic of aphorism types as they appear in *Terre des hommes*, one special case merits our brief attention. Fricke identifies a kind of aphorism that seeks to attack or to revise a well-established proverb, maxim, or a *lieu commun*. A fascinating case in point results from Saint-Exupéry's subtle revision of Nietzsche: "Et il ne s'agit point de vivre dangereusement. Cette formule est prétentieuse. Les toréadors ne me plaisent guère. Ce n'est pas le danger que j'aime. Je sais ce que j'aime. C'est la vie" (179). This is not to say, necessarily, that Saint-Exupéry undertook to respond directly to Nietzsche's watchword, enunciated in *Die fröhliche Wissenschaft* (1882). It had probably already become a commonplace saying, as it is today, by the time *Terre des hommes* was published in 1939. It is plausible that Saint-Exupéry was addressing himself to the *lieu commun* rather than to Nietzsche's original challenge.

Worth mentioning in passing: The original text from Nietzsche proves interesting: "Denn, glaubt es mir! – das Geheimnis, um die grösste Fruchtbarkeit und den grössten Genuss vom Dasein einzuernten, heisst: gefahrlich leben!" (So, believe me! – the secret of reaping the greatest rewards and the greatest pleasure from existence is: live dangerously! ii, 166:283, translation mine.)

THE WORLD OF THE TEXT

Employing the aphorisms of *Terre des hommes* in order to gain access to the "world" that the text attempts to project turns out to be little more than an echo of the numerous studies already done of Saint-Exupéry and his text. Indeed, perhaps unconsciously, critics most often use aphorisms in order to back up their various arguments.

Within this large body of criticism we encounter a high degree of duplication and overlapping. We need only consider a single recent study, Réal Ouellet's *Les Relations humaines dans l'œuvre de Saint-Exupéry*. Its chapter headings are emblematic of the themes that have been dealt with repeatedly:

"La Création, agent du devenir humain"
"La Création communautaire, fondement des relations humaines"
"L'Homme, être responsable," etc.

Assuredly, a reading of the chain of aphorisms in *Terre des hommes* reveals, in an extremely taut format, those mainsprings of the Exupérian corpus that have been repeatedly identified – to the point of annoyance – in the critical literature: selfhood (i.e., a Nietzschean "becoming what one is"), self-possession through creation and inter-action with the earth and its elements, personal and communal enrichment through working together for a common goal, a curious anti-materialism to be replaced by an emphasis on things "spiritual," the elusive nature of language, the utopian projection of a global/syncratic society, the ephemeral nature of existence, a spartan brand of love – and its corollary: a disdain for hollow pity or futile *attendrissement*, the Kierkegaardian belief in universal "essences" present in each human being. Any additional commentary on these themes would seem only to duplicate an overdeveloped body of scholarly work on the author and to trivialize further Saint-Exupéry's thought. From several of the aphorisms it is none the less possible to delve into two relatively unexplored areas of the Exupérian corpus and to venture a critique of them from a Marxist perspective. The two areas are loosely related.

In discussing Nietzsche and his philosophy, Geoffrey Clive speaks of the German thinker's "aristocratic radicalism," a term that could well – albeit to a milder extent – apply to Saint-Exupéry and his text. The *récits commentés*, or "equipment for living," that *Terre des hommes* proposes are for the most part founded on adventure, pioneering efforts, creation (as opposed to lacklustre repetition), existence on the verge of life and death, and steady doses of the Nietzschean "super-man" – all these mingled with tinges of epic revelry. At one point the text makes this isolated concession, however: "Nuits aériennes, nuits du désert ... ce sont là des occasions rares, qui ne s'offrent pas à tous les hommes ... J'ai trop parlé de quelques-uns et j'aimerais parler de tous" (192). The author-narrator does attempt, in the final pages of the novel, to universalize his heretofore elitist message – to "speak of one and all." However, as he observes the Polish masses huddled in a train, his observations and commentary seem to emanate from a privileged, perhaps condescending vantage-point (see 214–18).

A reading of the book's aphorisms, gathered together into a single list, supports the hypothesis that both narrator and, it follows, the text itself, tend to condescend to their reader. As regards the structural evidence to back up this premise, witness the fact that twenty or more of the work's aphorisms contain some form of superlative. Some fifteen others offer didactic, almost pretentious redefinitions of concepts ranging from "nostalgia" (201) to "truth" (206); still five others contain patronizing, didactic lexical elements such as "il faut" (160), "il ne faut pas" (205), and "il ne s'agit point" (217).

In a significant number of the book's aphorisms we witness also the recurrent appearance of "grand seigneur" imagery (e.g., 56, 191). The following sampling of such aristocratic reflections and the semantic elements that constitute them (the emphasis is added in each case) need no extraneous commentary:

L'empire de l'homme est intérieur.   (91)

Des hommes qui ont vécu longtemps d'un grand amour, puis en furent privés, se lassent parfois de leur noblesse solitaire. Ils se rapprochent humblement de la vie, et, d'un amour médiocre, font leur bonheur. Ils ont trouvé doux d'abdiquer, de se faire serviles, et d'entrer dans la paix des choses. L'esclave fait son orgueil de la braise du maître.   (116)

Mais il existe une altitude des relations où la reconnaissance comme la pitié perdent leur sens. C'est là que l'on respire comme un prisonnier délivré.   (201)

Saint-Exupéry's tendency towards high-flying escapism is an "equipment" – an attitude – embedded deep in his attempt through literature to project a radical humanism closely related to that of Nietzsche. This tendency might further be demonstrated by an almost stray aphorism made significant by its very marginality. Let us return to the fragment in the novel that appears as the narrator recounts his desperate situation in the middle of the African desert after the crash-landing. Here Saint-Exupéry "slips" by allowing himself to reflect on the possible time remaining until he dies. He abruptly interrupts his (and possibly also the reader's) reverie with "Mais il faut oublier certaines images" (160). With this injunction/aphorism the narrator scolds himself for thinking futile thoughts, and thereby indirectly admonishes his reader to do the same.

Saint-Exupéry's insistence on epic imperatives and his direct and indirect admonitions against succumbing to cowardly thoughts (such as those of death!) stand in subtle contrast to, for instance, Camus's or Gabrielle Roy's humanism. Indeed, these authors force their *personae* and their readers to confront and mentally assimilate the unsettling existential and social images Saint-Exupéry asks us to "forget," or to confront from a comfortable, elevated distance.

CONCLUSION

With regard to how aphorism is used in certain texts, *Terre des hommes* occupies a unique place among twentieth-century novels in French because of the tidy way it narrates actual epic events and interposes equal amounts of essayistic, "meditative" commentary. Most authors base their novels on imagined events and make a greater attempt to disguise their aphoristic formulations. Such blending of the two narrative functions – of reporting and evaluating – is often accomplished in other texts (1) by attributing the aphorism to the speech or thought of one of the characters, (2) by incorporating into the aphoristic sentence certain devices that fuse it to the narrated chain of events, or (3) by casting the verbs within such sentences into tenses other than the present, thereby causing them to seem to blend imperceptibly into the actual narration. Saint-Exupéry, by contrast, makes little or no effort to conceal his propensity for moralizing in the tradition of his seventeenth- and eighteenth-century countrymen.

Finally, perhaps no twentieth-century "francophone" novelist dares to write so didactically as Saint-Exupéry. The regular appearance of defining, attitudinizing, and admonishing aphorisms in the work make it something of an anachronism, a curious relic from the era of the *moralistes*. Nevertheless, the "world" conveyed by Saint-Exupéry's combination of *récits* and aphoristic commentary is a contemporary one, a world in which individual "wills to power" are impacted by bureaucratization, mechanization, the resurgence of totalizing, collective ideologies, poverty, and by the psychology of war. Saint-Exupéry proposes, as evidenced in the aphorisms of *Terre des hommes*, a humanist course of remedial action that attempts to fuse a highly individualistic, almost anarchistic ethic with syncratic values.

Drawing on his actual epic experience, Saint-Exupéry poses and attempts to answer the question "Que sera l'homme?" through literariness. In this particular case literariness may be defined as a clearly distinguishable intermingling of aphoristic "evaluation" and *récit*.

4 Alexandre Chenevert

An examination of the aphorisms in Gabrielle Roy's most substantial work, *Alexandre Chenevert*, brings to light a version of humanism akin to Saint-Exupéry's yet divergent from it in subtle but significant ways. Following *Terre des hommes* with *Alexandre Chenevert* in this study constitutes an interesting exercise, for Saint-Exupéry exerted considerable influence on Roy's thought and pen, and clear affinities exist between each of their bodies of writing.

In an interview conducted shortly before Roy's death, she declared: "I feel that I am a kindred spirit of Saint-Exupéry in the way that our writing is an echo both of our inner souls and of all humanity" (Delson-Karan, 198–9). Much of the vast corpus of secondary literature on Roy's writing mentions in some form the humanist foundation of her thought. For example, in an essay entitled "Tragic and Humanistic Visions of the Future," Paula Gilbert Lewis advances the view that "Roy's version of humanism [is] a feminine one, embracing the entire world." Lewis also proposes that humanism is the essential characteristic of a "world" author. On the basis of that definition she proceeds to rank Roy as a world-class writer and affirms that Roy "possesses [that] most fundamental gift" – that is, humanism (241).

Another Roy scholar, Paul Socken, proposes a reading of *Alexandre Chenevert* on two axes, a "horizontal" (or humanist- Marxist) one and a "vertical" (or mythical-metaphysical) one (8–9). Ben-Z. Shek's study

Social Realism in the French-Canadian Novel offers still another case in point. Shek deems *Alexandre Chenevert* a work of "deep humanism, stressing 'l'immensité enfermée dans (une) petite vie,' and of vital social criticism considerably in advance of the prevailing ideologies and announcing some of the fundamental changes in Quebec society that were to come later" (173).

Of indispensable aid to fathoming Gabrielle Roy's literary universe, and her brand of humanism, is the pivotal essay she was commissioned to write as an introduction to the 1967 World Exposition – Expo '67 – held in Montreal. Both the essay and the exposition were entitled "Terre des Hommes." This piece of writing, valuable as a summation/manifesto, also demonstrates Roy's direct links and natural affinity with Saint-Exupéry and his text. François Ricard concludes in his 1975 overview of Roy's life and work that the "Terre des Hommes" essay represents "un de [ses] écrits majeurs," and that "y sont annoncés l'inspiration et le climat de toute sa production récente, et que, d'autre part, ce texte représente comme l'aboutissement des grands thèmes qui avaient dominé les œuvres antérieures et leur transformation, leur 'objectivation' en une vaste vision du monde ou l'écrivain, comme réconcilié avec lui-même, étend à l'ensemble de l'univers les données et le sens de sa propre recherche" (128–9).

One can hardly overemphasize the importance of Roy's "Terre des Hommes" essay in the context of the present study, for it bristles with aphorisms and thus conclusively reveals her propensity for the genre. So it is not surprising to witness the regular appearance of the aphorism throughout her imaginative narrative prose.

Why might one select the less illustrious *Alexandre Chenevert* (1954) from among Roy's novels for an investigation of how she employs aphorism? Paul Socken (with Gérard Tougas) offers sufficiently good reason: "Gérard Tougas claims that *Alexandre Chenevert* is Gabrielle Roy's finest work, and perhaps the best in all of French-Canadian literature" (7). Further, Roy herself said of her character, some time after having drawn him: "Moi et Alexandre, nous ne sommes pas encore quittés" (Socken, 7). In his valuable interview with Socken in 1979, again only a few years before her death, Roy commented on the curious character she had drawn, and reaffirmed: "Chenevert surgit encore parfois devant moi pour se plaindre de ce que je n'ai pas tout dit de ses angoisses" (6). We will return to this interview to consider Roy's own interpretation of one of the book's key aphorisms.

Relatively little of the novel's aphoristic discourse appears to emanate from the authorial-narrative voice in the strict manner elaborated by Labov. Roy, as text-builder, instead works the great bulk of the book's aphorisms into the thought or speech of its main character, Alexandre Chenevert. This characterization thus deserves a few clarifying words and some background information before we embark on an examination of "his" aphoristic utterances and the role they might perform in the text.

To begin his interview, Paul Socken asked Roy whether she had read Georges Duhamel's "Salavin" series, to which she offered this response: "Yes, I certainly have. It was rather a long time before writing *Bonheur d'occasion*. Salavin struck me as truly the average man, torn between a natural egotism and goodness. It was very moving. It clarified for me the desire to create a character like Alexandre Chenevert" (92). We are thus confronted in the novel with an "Everyman" protagonist, albeit different from the lacklustre image one might conjure up of such a person, and certainly different from Salavin. Chenevert's claim to uniqueness resides in the fact that he reflects frequently – and profoundly – on his quest for personal salvation and a possible compassionate relationship with the rest of humanity.

Roy shed additional light on her enigmatic character in the form of a commentary on the statement she had made to Ben Shek some years earlier (i.e., "Alexandre et moi nous ne sommes pas encore quittés"): "I don't know what makes Alexandre act the way he does. I created him, but I do not fully understand him. A part of him escapes me. He remains somewhat of a mystery, an enigma. Like you, I keep seeking Alexandre Chenevert. I know who Florentine, Azarius and my other characters are, but not Alexandre. He is too complex, too rich" (93).

One might safely extrapolate from Roy's statements on Chenevert her sense of sympathy and personal identification with the character she created. If we couple this identification with a telling argument put forward by the critic Gilles Marcotte – namely, that Chenevert "reste un thème plutôt qu'un homme" (Socken, 8) – we might reasonably deduce that Chenevert – "his" thoughts open to us "like a book" – forms a closely related extension of the novel's overtly authorial, third-person narrative voice. Additionally, Chenevert is the only character in the book whom we know to be leading an examined, self-conscious life. His concentrated, often aphoristic thoughts and utterances therefore demand special attention on the part of the reader, and call for analysis.

In Appendix B, those aphorisms that emanate from the authorial-narrative voice are marked by stars. All others are ostensibly the thought/expression of "Chenevert," Roy's shorthand symbol for the average person who is striving to strike a balance between at least three opposing forces: an egotistical "will to power," a collective sensibility, and the quest for some sense of personal salvation.

THE NARRATOLOGICAL CONSEQUENCE OF APHORISM

The narrator of *Alexandre Chenevert* only occasionally interrupts the flow of her *récit* to interpolate an aphorism blatantly in the manner of Saint-Exupéry. Let us focus on a typical case in point. The context is one of Chenevert's moments of extended reflection – at times bigoted, at times compassionate – on humanity at large. In this instance his intentionality is directed towards the Japanese, their attack on Pearl Harbor, and the notion of "Made in Japan." An extraneous voice breaks in with no forewarning, as an "evaluation" of, and subtle counterfoil to, Chenevert's thought: "Sans les morts, les absents, les peuplades jamais visitées, que deviendrait chez l'homme la faculté d'aimer!" (21)

This partly rhetorical question/aphorism, elliptically presented to round off a lengthy reverie sequence, must have puzzled Paul Socken – as it would most readers. He therefore asked Roy to explain:

[Socken:] Sans les morts, les absents … In what way may one understand that comment?
[Roy:] We tend to love people who are far away, or inaccessible. Once they're dead it's even safer to love them. When a person has been gone for six months, he becomes good. We take for granted the loved one who is close. All their faults seem to bother us. It all points out the difficulty we have in loving one another. We don't feel the weight of those who are no longer with us.   (93)

However, the novel tends to avoid obvious interventions of this kind. Instead, it favours aphoristic strands woven into the general fabric of the work. Indeed, the text abounds with fragments of evaluative, generalizing commentary, intermingled with the narrative. Consider this representative paragraph:

Lui aussi [Chenevert], bien entendu, menait une vie de fou: des repas avalés en vitesse à des heures irrégulières, un sommeil souvent interrompu, la responsabilité, voilà ce qui usait le plus. Cedependant, il ne pouvait guère faire autrement que vivre ce qui était sa vie après tout.   (168)

When the author-narrator attributes either reflective thought to her "Monsieur tout-le-monde" (see "la responsabilité, voilà ce qui us[e] le plus") or injects editorial commentary (see "il ne pouvait guère faire autrement) into the narration, she tends throughout the novel to assign markers of the imperfect tense to the relevant verbs. This specialized deployment of the imperfect has the effect of rendering the temporal locus of such reflective thoughts so imprecise that they become effectively as timeless as verbs cast in the present tense. Roy frequently shapes her characterization of Chenevert – whom we may regard as a literary transposition of the post–Second World War "common man" – by placing him in universally recognizable situations (see "des repas avalés en vitesse"). These workaday scenes, common to the middle and working classes of Western civilization, often have the effect of lulling the reader into replacing, quite unconsciously, the "il" of the narrative with "on" or even with "je."

In creating a listing of the novel's aphorisms, I have not extensively reworked any of these generic "strands" in an effort to make them capable of standing alone – that is, in isolation from the text. Nevertheless, many of "Chenevert's" aphoristic thoughts require only that a word or two of introduction be stripped away and their verb(s) be given present-tense markers for them to exist as independent texts.

Compare, as an illustration of this method, the original thought with the slightly modified version. The verb marker is altered so that it indicates the durative present:

Et il [Chenevert] en fut, ce soir, à se demander avec sérieux s'il ne valait pas mieux en ce monde être malade plutôt que malheureux.   (110)

Ne vaut-il pas mieux en ce monde être malade plutôt que malheureux[?]

Chenevert, the bank teller, stretches the limits of our belief in him as a real character, for he reasons in a keen, often highly philosophical mode, as evidenced by this appendage to the story-line: "Au fond, l'expérience amère qu'il avait aujourd'hui à offrir [to his daughter, Elise] était celle-là même qu'il avait en son temps dédaignée. *En allait-il jamais autrement de l'expérience, vérité somme toute incommunicable?*" (65, emphasis added)

Such reflections seem almost to have been imported from an exterior set of "philosophical investigations" and given expression through the agency of Chenevert. Perhaps Marcotte, too, discerned the workings of this phenomenon and for this reason was led to regard Chenevert more as a "thème" than a person familiar to us in the referential world. However, we do well to bear in mind that a tautology results from the question of whether or not the concentrated idea, "l'expérience, vérité somme toute incommunicable" is an authorial intervention or the thought of Alexandre Chenevert. In the final analysis the entire text, characters and all, came into being through their author, Gabrielle Roy.

As tightly interwoven as all the narratological elements are in this text, it seems a useful exercise to become keenly aware of the novel's essential bits of "Denkökonomie." In order to access this text's unusual "world" and its possible "proverb writ large," it is particularly interesting to review the large number of barely disguised aphorisms that Roy attributes to the thought and expression of Alexandre Chenevert.

This is not to imply that within the work only the voice of Chenevert utters generic statements. The generalizing utterances that emanate from other sources, though relatively less frequent, also call for analysis as one attempts to make sense of the novel. I have chosen not to list or study these separately, however, for in most cases they prove to be trite *lieux communs* called into question by the more "antagonistic" aphorisms of either Chenevert or the novel's editorial voice. Perhaps the following cases – two of many in the text – most aptly demonstrate the text's rebuttal of commonplace expression and, ultimately, of the unexamined thought that propagates hackneyed constructs.

At one point in the narration the director of Alexandre's bank, M. Fontaine, deems it necessary to offer some words of remedial advice to his subordinate. Roy first reveals that the director's *livre de chevet* is *Comment réussir dans la vie et se faire des amis* (90). The counsel Fontaine offers Chenevert, not surprisingly, breathes banality:

– Play hard ... work hard;
– Ne perdez pas une minute de temps et le temps vous appartiendra;
– Maintenez-vous en bonne santé, et la vie vous paraîtra digne d'être vécue. (90)

The first statement, an incidence of code-switching from the usual French into English, might be viewed as a pointed manifestation of the pressure that North American, anglophone culture exerts on francophone-Canadian civilization.

At a later point in the novel Chenevert, the North American Everyman, is subjected to the advertising industry and its barrage of vacuous clichés: "Il fut livré aux annonces qui d'un bout à l'autre du tram, au-dessus des banquettes, prodiguaient des conseils, des menaces, des avertissements. Le jello *yum-yum* était incomparable ... *et le seul isme pour les Canadiens*, exprimait une distillerie, *était le Patriotisme*" (272).

To sum up the narratological behaviour of aphorisms in *Alexandre Chenevert*, we have remarked that the novel consists only partially of narrative and readily distinguishable bits of aphoristic commentary. Gabrielle Roy clearly diverges from the narrative strategy we observed in *Terre des hommes*. Instead, she tends to place evaluative and aphoristic formulations into the consciousness and speech of the main character, Alexandre Chenevert – whom she felt unable to "leave." Finally, the close reader of this text witnesses a dialogue – a subtle combat – between the *lieux communs* of North American civilization and an opposing set of more thoughtful generic utterances that challenge the first.

INSIGHTS GAINED FROM A SEPARATE LISTING OF THE NOVEL'S APHORISMS

A significant number of the aphorisms used in this novel contain, either separately or in concert, the easily identifiable, interrelated devices of antithesis, irony, oxymoron, and zeugma:

Alliés, ennemis, alliés ...   (14)

[Est]-ce donc inévitablement par ce qu'on aim[e] le moins en *soi* que l'on rest[e] si bien lié *aux autres*?   (51, emphasis added)

Le *malheur* paraît *alléger* le poids familier de la vie.   (129, emphasis added)

This frequent use of opposing terms offers structural evidence of Roy's lifelong effort to demonstrate through literature what she perceived to be the fundamental quality of existence – namely, the presence of warring desires and emotions within the subjective. The title of her last work, the autobiographical *La Détresse et l'Enchantement*, testifies clearly to Roy's penchant for inscribing opposing desires and emotions.

Akin to such "ironic" discourse, which seeks to unite contradictory terms through lingual means, is the kind of expression that relies on a more elusive *pointe* for its effect. Consider, first, this general illustration of Roy's tendency in the novel to expose human foibles with remarks that are at once benevolent and mordant: "Pour s'entendre entre mari et femme, entre collègues, entre amis, avec n'importe qui, entre les peuples, aux conférences de paix il ne d[oit] y avoir que ce moyen: le silence" (117). The surprise appearance of "silence" at the end of the aphorism, proffered as a sarcastic solution to the lack of harmony between people, is not difficult to analyse.

More elusive to hard analysis are certain subtleties of tone and the production of emotion that emanate from the accumulation of simple yet enigmatic semantic loads. It takes little to recognize how the above piece of text first evokes the usual remedies, then mocks the fact that they have continually failed. A more complex question, though, is how subtle emotions – for example, irritation, guilt, a slight sense of despair – are produced from otherwise insignificant building-blocks.

Let us review another instance of Roy's penchant – at least in this novel – for subtle derision through the use of a pithy, ironic obser-vation: "A se grouper ... étroitement, les médecins donnent l'impres-sion d'être très forts contre la douleur" (109). In this case we observe no elements constitutive of antithesis or the empirically observable device of irony. Instead, we are simply presented with a caricature of the medical profession and a hint of ridicule at their grouping together in order to create the illusion that they are "strong" in their ability to combat "pain." If the reader takes the time to reflect further, the text goes on to imply that we succumb to the deception, thinking that we can somehow succeed in transferring our pain on to the therapist. One reason we might think it possible is that the closely knit group seems so big, and therefore powerful.

In still another variation on the leitmotiv of benevolent yet none the less mordant censure of human foibles, witness the series of semantic displacements that the word "amour" can undergo in this terse example: "Combien triste est l'amour au confessionnal!" (325)

All the aphorisms described above might be fused into a single broad category of generic *irony*. The term in this case characterizes less the empirically definable rhetorical device than an attempt in Roy's text to bring together heretofore contradictory terms. One might say that irony more broadly defined in this way represents the coherence strategy for the whole of *Alexandre Chenevert*.

As we consider the book's aphorisms, we find that Roy often supplements this overarching approach with a wide range of apho-ristic devices enumerated by Fricke. To name some of them:

- The frequent use of language made provocative through hyper-bole: "On est *toujours* mieux à deux pour être content. Même un chien connaît cela" (226, emphasis added).
- The repeated employment of interrogative devices (roughly one-third of the aphorisms listed pose either a rhetorical or an open-ended question): "Et si c'était tout simplement pour ne plus voir souffrir la moitié du temps que Dieu avait décidé de ce tour de la terre autour du soleil?" (211)

- The frequent tendency towards highly subtle "definitions": for example, "cette sorte de brusquerie qui t[ient] lieu de charité" (173).

Although irony in its generic sense represents a kind of master text-building strategy in *Alexandre Chenevert*, it would be erroneous to say that Roy excludes other tones. A smaller yet significant number of aphoristic sentences in this novel display no trace of paradox or banter and thereby bear structural witness to an even more fundamental tone in the text – namely, unabashed sobriety. One example represents well this entire group: "Que d'impressions heureuses en un seul jour peuvent donc pénétrer un cœur humain, lorsqu'il est libre de les accueillir!" (224)

A final remark on Roy's use of the revisionary aphorism is in order. Within some of the novel's aphorisms themselves we witness a concise manifestation of her aim, evident throughout *Alexandre Chenevert*, to debunk the hackneyed *lieux communs* of Western, and particularly North American civilization: "'Voyez les lis des champs et les oiseaux …' Très bien, mais ni les oiseaux mangeurs d'insectes, ni les lis abreuvés d'eau de pluie n'avaient à prévoir leur propre enterrement" (364). Then: "Si je n'ai rien à gagner, je n'ai rien à perdre" (152). The first example revises conventional biblical wisdom, the second the overworked notion of "nothing ventured, nothing gained."

On the question of whether Roy's writing fits into the "integrative" tradition of the French moralists or the "antagonistic" mold of the German reflective philosophers, we observe a blending of the two modes in her work. To be sure, certain isolated aphorisms within *Alexandre Chenevert* can be analysed as purely integrative or purely antagonistic. Most of them, however, while antagonistic in tone and style, comment on usual situations and human foibles in the real world, in the manner of La Bruyère, La Rochefoucauld, et al.

THE WORLD OF THE TEXT

As was the case with Saint-Exupéry's *Terre des hommes*, a look at the aphorisms in *Alexandre Chenevert* often serves to confirm the presence in Roy's work of themes that have already been dealt with, exhaustively, in the critical literature. In other words, the aphorisms reveal no major preoccupations that have not already been adequately brought to light. First and foremost of these concerns is Roy's constant oscillation between opposing poles, and her ability to effect a synthesis only through the symbolic medium of literature.

On this issue François Ricard takes one of Roy's remarks, recorded in *Le Devoir*, 18 May 1974, and makes it the leitmotiv of his 1975 overview of her life and work. Accordingly, the quotation is featured prominently as the epigraph to his entire study: "Je cherche encore à concilier le besoin de liberté dont nous ne pouvons nous passer avec l'affection qui attache, la tendresse qui retient, les liens de solidarité qui ne doivent se défaire. Et voilà notre vie! Nous voulons les opposés, les inconciliables. Et arrange-toi comme tu peux entre tes désirs qui s'entre-déchirent" (8). Such sets of oppositions in Roy's text – and the one mentioned above between the individual and the collective is fundamental – often become imbued in *Alexandre Chenevert* with a kind of rueful irony/sarcasm. The omnipresence in the text of this tone serves to indicate how Roy perceives the human project to be perhaps more precarious than epic.

It may be useful to mention in passing that two notable contemporary French thinkers, Alain Renault and Luc Ferry, have published recent analyses of the post-Heideggerian wave of "antihumanisme" in Western civilization. In the process they provocatively suggest a re-evaluation, revision, and possible revival of traditional humanist ideals. Like Gabrielle Roy, they posit a balance between unbridled, narcissistic individualism and collective concerns. All the while, however, they fully acknowledge, as does Roy, the failure in Western civilization ever to realize an equilibrium between the two. Through philosophical-rhetorical means Renault cautiously asks for a rehabilitation of traditional humanism. He terms the modified approach, proposed not overtly but between the lines of his philosophical treatise, "un humanisme non individualiste" (52–62). This revision of Nietzschean humanism characterizes well the kind of humanism Roy posits throughout all her texts, but particularly in *Alexandre Chenevert*.

Some of the other thematic concerns dealt with in the secondary literature, and exhibited in the aphorisms of *Alexandre Chenevert*, are Roy's recurrent articulation of "the drama between man and God" (Socken 92); her idiosyncratic views on "solitude"; her conception of writing and the act of reading as an attempt at intersubjective communion; her quest for individual selfhood and "salvation"; her belief in salutary, tutorial suffering; her vision of a syncratic world.

One area of research remains relatively untouched, however. Roy's writings have only infrequently provided raw material for study from a feminist perspective. Several of the aphorisms in *Alexandre Chenevert*, of which the two below stand out, support the contention that Roy's texts constitute an untapped resource for discussion of feminist issues (303): "Ces ennuis de santé communs à un certain age de la femme, pour ainsi dire naturels, sans grand intérêt, néanmoins aussi lourds peut-être à supporter que d'autres pour lesquels il y a de la sympathie" (113). "Les hommes et les femmes sur terre [sont] irrémédiablement isolés les uns des autres par les misères particulières à leur sexe et qu'à tout prendre celles des femmes [sont] peut-être les plus lourdes" (127).

Newcomers to Roy's writing may wonder about her stance on Québec nationalism. In this regard she is known to have had federalist leanings, and she sought solutions to Canada's problems of national identity mainly from a humanist/syncratic vantage-point. None the less, she proved a strong advocate for the linguistic and cultural rights of francophone Canadians. Two of *Alexandre Chenevert*'s generic utterances succinctly allude to her at once uncompromising and conciliatory attitude towards the two founding peoples of Canada: "L'Anglais ..., c'[est] l'ennemi héréditaire, proposé par l'histoire, l'école, l'entourage, celui dont [on] pourrait à peine se passer, tant, en le perdant, ses griefs manqueraient d'emploi" (19). "En français, en anglais, toujours, il faut bien, car on est dans une ville [Montréal] qui pense et souffre en deux langues" (308).

Finally, the aphorisms of Roy's third novel, viewed as a separate group, show just how rich in subtle, discriminating ideas the text proves to be. Consider only these four. The discussion centres around, respectively, the locus of "truth" within the morass of writings created by civilization, the widespread inability to express affection except through neurotic channels, the unlikely (but highly provocative) thought that a connection exists between sleep and independence, and the paradox of pain-relieving drugs:

l'homme moderne hérit[e] d'une montagne de connaissances. ... Et où est la vérité, dans cette masse d'écrits? (23)

Tant de gens sur terre n'arrivent à exprimer leur affection que par l'inquiétude. (150)

Par le sommeil Dieu consentait que sa créature arrivât de temps en temps à se croire indépendante. (211)

La drogue ... [avec] son pouvoir dissolvant ... n'est-elle pas, hors la douleur, le plus énigmatique cadeau fait par Dieu aux hommes? (341–2)

For the purposes of classroom or schorlarly treatment, such compact bits of backgrounded thought constitute a network of minor themes within the novel. They can provide tidy points of departure for hermeneutical or more ideologial – for example, Marxist-oriented –

treatment. Many of these subsidiary themes have been ignored or neglected by the critics and await scholarly attention.

However, in all our academic zeal to dissect, we may do well to remind ourselves that these fragments of concentrated thought are woven into the "mystery" (Socken, 93) of the novel's protagonist – into his actions, words, and thoughts – and in the final analysis are inseparable from the characterizations and from the narrated thoughts and actions.

CONCLUSION

One could safely classify *Alexandre Chenevert* as a highly aphoristic piece of writing both by the numerical frequency of appearance of the genre and by the generic and eminently provocative quality of the entire text. Were these compressed reflections omitted, the reader might be tempted, as was Ollendorf with Proust's manuscript, to wonder how an author could continue for 384 pages to describe a man who appeared to demand nothing more from life than "son frigidaire enfin payé, un gagne-pain assuré et un habit neuf tous les deux ans" (18).

It is through the reader's ability to access at least some of the operations of Chenevert's reflective consciousness, which Roy often expresses through the agency of pithy aphoristic formulation, that an otherwise lacklustre character becomes memorable and rich.

We have observed how the aphoristic reflections of Chenevert, some of them crafted with obvious care, are often indistinguishable from those of the anonymous narrative voice. Through the master trope of irony Roy uses the genre of aphorism at once to criticize prevalent attitudes and to demonstrate (and perhaps rue) the incongruity of her lofty ideals with the onerous reality of the quotidian. In Roy's world "myth and morality" are fused, for the time being, only through the medium of literature. Aphorism constitutes one of the main points of juncture in her text between such irreconcilable opposites.

5 *Gouverneurs de la rosée*

In a study subtitled the "Life and Work of Jacques Roumain" Carolyn Fowler consolidates key information from a disparate secondary literature, examines significant new primary sources, and conducts interviews in order to provide a reliable overview of the Haitian author's career. She echoes a unified critical view that Roumain's final work, *Gouverneurs de la rosée*, represents a synthesis and a pinnacle within his literary production (248–9, 253–4).

With regard to the use of aphorism in this text Fowler recognizes that Roumain intervenes in all his narrative fiction to "inject doctrine," but particularly in *Gouverneurs de la rosée*. Her observations on this topic offer a convenient introduction to the various issues addressed in this more specialized study:

These themes, of the revolt of the damned of the earth, of man's reward through his own efforts, of human solidarity and the liberation of the mind from superstition are, in the final analysis, simply various aspects of the same essential theme of human betterment. They are broached many times during the course of the story as Manuel [the protagonist of *Gouverneurs de la rosée*] speaks with one or another of the characters, or as he reflects on his hopes for the future. It is this aspect of the novel which has caused some critics to speak of Roumain's tendency to editorialize and to inject his Marxist doctrines into the novel.   (237)

Fowler then presents several illustrations of such "editorializing." Each can be analysed as an aphorism. Fowler notes that such passages often prove to be simple transpositions of Roumain's essayistic writings, composed earlier (237). She then concludes that, "although the editorializing in these passages may be somewhat distracting, the full effect of Manuel's words and thoughts lies in the fact that they are repeated after his death by those in whose company he spoke them" (237). One might add that the reason his "words and thoughts" are memorable is that they are aphoristic and eminently capable of "slipping off the tongue," in the words of John Gross.

Fowler also brings to light key influences that helped to shape Roumain's thought and writing. Some of these influences bear on his attraction to aphorism as a fitting genre for transmitting his thought. Having completed a significant portion of his studies in Bern and Zürich, Roumain became intimately familiar during his formative years with the highly aphoristic writings of Nietzsche (3, 7). Later, in the Haiti of the 1930s, Roumain followed the pattern set by other intellectuals of his country, who looked to Marx for their ideological inspiration (144). The work of these two thinkers clearly informs *Gouverneurs de la rosée* with regard to both the novel's form and its substance.

One final biographical detail that Fowler documents deserves mention here, for it casts further light on the aphoristic elements in *Gouverneurs de la rosée*. At the age of eighteen, while in Europe, Roumain wrote in a letter to the editor of Haiti's opposition newspaper: "J'ai hâte de retourner en Haïti, afin d'aider à relever le courage des masses et à soulager le peuple" (7).

In the chapter of Fowler's book entitled "Mobilizing the Haitian Masses and a New Use for Literature," she suggests that Roumain's early aspirations were realized principally in the act of writing, that he conceived literature as a means "to interpret Marxist theory to a Haitian audience" (149). So one might construe *Gouverneurs de la rosée*, with its frequent interjections of concentrated philosophical thought, as Roumain's most polished attempt to achieve his youthful aspirations.

THE NARRATOLOGICAL CONSEQUENCE OF APHORISM

To a more obvious extent than Gabrielle Roy's *Alexandre Chenevert*, Manuel, the protagonist of *Gouverneurs de la rosée*, becomes a literary transposition of the author's thought. One might say that Manuel is caused to act for and on behalf of Roumain. The parallels between Manuel and the author who created him are immediately evident: Manuel's dramatic return to his native land, having learned another language and undergone a transformatory apprenticeship; the fact that both return to their country more sharply aware of and disturbed by their compatriots' propensity for superstitious resignation; their common desire to offer a remedy to the adverse situation; the Nietzschean "excès de vie" exhibited by both figures (Fowler, 253); the messianic – that is, Zarathustrian – aura that each creates around himself.

Roumain postpones Manuel's first appearance in the novel until well into the narrative (25). In the section of the text leading up to that appearance, very little sententiousness emanates from the narrator. These few utterances prove to be in complete harmony, however, with the Zarathustrian pronouncements of Manuel that are to follow.

Indeed, an aphorism initiates the novel: "Nous mourrons tous" (11). What at first blush seems to be a cliché sets the tone of the entire novel by evoking the need to face hard realities, ultimately death itself. It is this idea, arguably, that lends coherence to the entire narrated chain of events.

A few lines later there follows a corollary to this first aphorism, in the form of a commentary on one of the reported events. Manuel's mother, Délira, has been invoking "le bon Dieu." The narrator intervenes didactically: "Mais c'est inutile, parce qu'il y a si tellement beaucoup de pauvres créatures qui hèlent le bon Dieu de tout leur courage que ça fait un grand bruit ennuyant et le bon Dieu l'entend et il crie: Quel est, foutre, tout ce bruit? Et il bouche les oreilles. C'est la vérité et l'homme est abandonné" (11).

Otherwise, the book's aphoristic utterances and reflections emerge, with some exceptions, particularly at the end of the text, from the characterization named Manuel. One of these is worth noting at this stage, for Roumain often marks his "editorial" interventions in order to introduce them. In this case he uses a dash to carry out this "marking" function: "Ce n'était pas seulement le besoin de repos: la houe devenant de plus en plus lourde à manier, le joug de la fatigue sur la nuque raide, l'échauffement du soleil; c'est que le travail finissait. Pourtant on s'était à peine arrêté, le temps d'avaler une gorgée de tafia, de se détendre les reins – *dans le corps c'est ce qu'il y a de plus récalcitrant, les reins*" (19, emphasis added).

Manuel's quasi-scriptural sentences – delivered in a somewhat condescending manner reminiscent of the Nietzschean Zarathustra – emerge quite naturally, usually during the course of a conversation with another of the book's characters. We need only view one or two relevant situations in order to grasp the technique.

In the narrative sequence where Manuel first meets Annaise, the topic of conversation turns to "les tribulations de l'existence" (29). The narrator reports how Manuel begins to speak, "les poings fermés," and how he proceeds to redefine, didactically and philosophically, the concept of *rage* for his interlocutor: "La rage. La rage te fait serrer les mâchoires et boucler ta ceinture plus près de la peau de ton ventre quand tu as faim. La rage, c'est une grande force" (29). One might consider this statement to be a concentrated, popularized version of Nietzsche's idea of the "will to power."

In another sequence towards the end of the novel, in the interim between Manuel's being stabbed and his subsequent death, the protagonist offers this final piece of advice to his mother: "Vous avez offert des sacrifices aux loa, vous avez offert le sang des poules et des cabris pour faire tomber la pluie, ça n'a servi à rien. *Parce que ce qui compte, c'est le sacrifice de l'homme. C'est le sang du nègre*" (760, emphasis added). Fowler points out, using the example above, that after Manuel's death Délira easily recalls and repeats her son's pithy, didactic sentences (238).

However, the other characters are not content simply to mouth the utterances of their "Général Manuel" (131); rather, through him they have themselves attained a certain enlightenment and authenticity. They themselves now display an ability to think critically and to express their thought effectively. As evidence of this evolution we observe in their own aphoristic utterances a new-found capacity to reflect on and evaluate phenomena around them.

With analytical acumen Antoine demolishes a facile *lieu commun*: "Le Bondieu est bon, dit-on. Le Bondieu est blanc, qu'il faudrait dire. Et peut-être que c'est tout juste le contraire" (165).

Annaise exhibits keen skills of observation, an ability to look past the immediately obvious and think dialectically, and then arrive at a balanced conclusion: "Les plantes, c'est comme les chrétiens. Il y en a de deux qualités: les bonnes et les mauvaises. Quand tu vois des oranges, tous ces petits soleils accrochés dans le feuillage, tu sens comme une réjouissance, c'est plaisant et c'est serviable, les oranges. Tandis que, prends une plante à piquants comme celle-là … Mais, il ne faut rien maudire parce que c'est le bon Dieu qui a tout crée" (191).

Even Délira, once enmeshed in all the trappings of metaphysical resignation and superstition, not only comes to understand the possible benefits of her son's "godless" (in the Niezschean sense) ethic but also begins to discern for herself the value of "simplicity, frankness, and honesty" in her neighbours (17).

In sum, the aphorisms of *Gouverneurs de la rosée* are to be found mainly in the reported speech of the novel's characters and particularly in the utterances of the protagonist, Manuel. Only exceptionally do they emanate from the narrative voice or from the reported thought of the characters. An analysis of these utterances reveals how the novel's messianic protagonist endeavours to better the lot of those around him and how the other characters respond in varying ways to his injunctions.

INSIGHTS GAINED FROM A SEPARATE LISTING OF THE NOVEL'S APHORISMS

An overview of all the novel's aphorisms reveals a near absence of rhetorical artifice, of "pointes," or of subtle dialectical elements; instead, Roumain tends to convey simple, readily understandable propositions through the agency of a protagonist who in the text is direct and readily understood by the uneducated classes. Manuel's aphoristic formulations, therefore, most often take the form of fairly straightforward definitions – for example, of "le malheur" (12), "la rage" (29), "la consolation" (29–30), "la vie" (34), "la résignation" (47), etc.

In addition to Manuel's idiosyncratic definition of "la rage," viewed previously, a single additional example will suffice to illustrate this relatively uncomplicated technique of redefinition: "C'est traître, la résignation; c'est du pareil au même que le découragement. Ça vous casse les bras: on attend les miracles et la Providence, chapelet en main, sans rien faire" (47).

Occasionally, as Roumain constructs such "definition" aphorisms, he will resort to the additional device of archetypal metaphors from nature or everyday life in order to represent otherwise obscure abstractions: He employs "arbre" to represent "un être vivant" (18); "le fruit," life and death (34); "le lait caillé," a trivial matter (109), etc.

However, Roumain's aim to define and to put a particular slant on familiar concepts surpasses the desire merely to educate his interlocutor in some empirical way. On the contrary, Manuel's aphoristic observations, despite being reformulated in everyday language and in familiar images, may be viewed as deceptively profound philosophical investigations:

Et il *n'y a d'autre* Providence que son travail d'habitant sérieux; d'autre miracle que le fruit de ses mains.   (47, emphasis added)

Les compliments, *ça ne sert à rien et ce n'est pas nécessaire.* (82, emphasis added)

Stendhal, in *Le Rouge et le Noir*, explores the idea of Providence in much the same way. The word is also capitalized throughout his text. However, Stendhal's investigation requires a much higher degree of sophistication on the part of the reader even to grasp its initial meaning, much less its multifaceted nuances. It is also surprising, at first glance, that Roumain would introduce the idea of flattery and compliments into an otherwise gritty discussion informed by Marxist realism. Upon closer reflection, however, the subtle interrelation between hard work to accomplish a difficult goal and the uselessness of compliments emerges.

We also observe through the examples cited above how complex and polyvalent ideas are often introduced in the novel with primitive – yes, overtly didactic – phrases, such as "c'est comme ça" (29), " tu as beau" (34), "ce qui compte" (84, 150, 185), "la vie est faite pour que" (99), "c'est ça qui" (113), "faut que" (134), "tu sais pourquoi?" (191), and "parce que" (160).

THE WORLD OF THE TEXT

A perusal of the aphorisms scattered throughout *Gouverneurs de la rosée* readily indicates the Marxian substance of the novel. We need not analyse this aspect of the work in any detail, for it has been thoroughly identified and discussed in the critical literature. A few brief evocations of this substance, captured neatly in the book's aphorisms, will suffice as a complement to Carolyn Fowler's summarizing remarks.

She contrasts Pierre, the protagonist of an earlier novel, with Manuel of *Gouverneurs de la rosée*: "In 'Le champs du potier,' Pierre, unlike his predecessors, has risen above personalities. He sees the people about him and their values in the light of class conditioning. His constant musings establish a tension in the human condition between individual desires and historical process. The struggle in 'Gouverneurs de la rosée' appears to be on both the historical and the essential human levels. The hero's dilemma arises from the tension created between the two levels" (247).

Fowler's remarks also rightly speak to another dimension, namely "the essential human levels" of the novel. Fowler does not elaborate, nor does the critical literature pay any significant attention to the human – that is, the individual – level.

As regards the first, or the Marxian level in the following aphorism, we observe clear allusions to class struggle. It serves as a clear and concise manifestation of the text's solidarity with the poorer classes, its rebuttal of metaphysical solutions, and its advocacy of materialist remedies:

Il y a les affaires du ciel et il y a les affaires de la terre: ça fait deux et ce n'est pas la même chose. Le ciel, c'est le pâturage des anges; ils sont bienheureux; ils n'ont pas à prendre soin du manger et du boire. Et sûrement qu'il y a des anges nègres pour faire le gros travail de la lessive des nuages ou balayer la pluie et mettre la propreté du soleil après l'orage, pendant que les anges blancs chantent comme des rossignols toute la sainte journée ou bien soufflent dans de petites trompettes comme c'est marqué dans les images qu'on voit dans les églises.

Mais la terre, c'est une bataille jour pour jour, une bataille sans repos: défricher, planter, sarcler, arroser, jusqu'à la récolte, et alors tu vois ton champ mûr couché devant toi le matin, sous la rosée, et l'orgueil entre dans ton cœur. (37)

From another of the book's host of "defining" aphorisms emerges evidence of Roumain's penchant for collective solutions: "la grève c'est ça: un NON de mille voix qui ne font qu'une et qui s'abat sur la table du patron avec le pesant d'une roche" (86).

Then, in this string, or "chain," of aphorisms – respecting the text's own sequencing – we witness literary expression of the Marxian views on solidarity, labour, and "historical" progress:

Chaque nègre pendant son existence y fait un nœud: c'est le travail qu'il a accompli et c'est ça qui rend la vie vivante dans les siècles des siècles: l'utilité de l'homme sur cette terre. (113)

Sans la concorde la vie n'a pas de goût, la vie n'a pas de sens. (127)

On ne peut pas avaler une grappe de raisin d'un seul coup, mais grain par grain, c'est facile. (126)

Now let us take a closer look at Roumain the humanist. In this regard, Roumain's world of ideas is demonstrably Nietzschean, although this "world" overlaps considerably with that of Marx. This is not, however, to suggest that Roumain transposes Nietzsche into his last novel as clearly as he transposes Marx. Identifying Nietzschean intertext in Roumain's work proves far more difficult and has not been undertaken to any significant degree in the critical literature. However, Roumain's "passion" for Nietzsche is indisputable. He wrote in a 1922 letter from Grünau: "La seule chose que je fasse avec passion est la lecture: Schopenhauer, Nietzsche, Darwin et les vers de Heine et de Lenau" (Fowler, 3).

Nietzsche's shorthand symbols, which now enjoy wide currency in Western civilization, allow convenient and efficient discussion of the ground-breaking ideas that he aimed to convey. The parallels, whether deliberately intertextual or born of affinity, between *Gouverneurs de la rosée* and Nietzsche's writings prove enlightening. As a beginning example, let us again view Roumain's concept, expressed in a "definition" aphorism, of rage: "La rage te fait serrer les mâchoires et boucler ta ceinture plus près de la peau de ton ventre quand tu as faim. La rage c'est une grande force" (29).

The idea of "rage" as a "force" recalls Nietzsche's spin on the French word *ressentiment,* or the "will to revenge" (Schlechta II, 232). For Nietzsche, ressentiment constitutes a major determinant in the formation of individual and collective "wills to power." He expresses the idea perhaps as concisely as anywhere in *Zur Genealogie der Moral*:

With regard to morals, the slave insurrection begins with "ressentiment" itself becoming creative and giving birth to new values: ... While all aristocratic morals grow out of a triumphant affirmation of oneself, slave morality rejects from the outset "exterior circumstances," "foreign existence," that which is not one's own: and this rejection is its ["slave" morality's] creative act.

Slave morality always requires, in order to manifest itself, first a counter-world, an outside world; it requires, physiologically speaking, outside stimuli in order to act at all – its actions are fundamentally reactions.   (II, 782, translation mine)

As a further example, it is very tempting to observe in Manuel's poetic, quasi-scriptural discourse on "the earth" a Zarathustrian foundation. Compare Roumain's creation, Manuel, to the Nietzschean Zarathustra and note the similarities in their discourse on the same topic:

En vérité, il y a une consolation, je vais te dire: c'est la terre, ton morceau de terre fait pour le courage de tes bras, avec tes arbres fruitiers à l'entour, tes bêtes dans le pâturage, toutes tes nécessités à portée de la main et ta liberté qui n'a pas une autre limite que la saison bonne ou mauvaise, la pluie ou la sécheresse. (*Gouverneurs,* 29–30)

Remain true to the earth, my brethren, with the power of your virtue! Let your bestowing love and your knowledge be devoted to the meaning of the earth! Thus I do pray and conjure you.

Let it not fly away from the earthly and beat against eternal walls with its wings! Ah, there hath always been so much flown-away virtue!

Lead, like me, the flown-away virtue back to the earth – yea, back to body and life: that it may give to the earth its meaning, a human meaning!

A thousand paths are there which have never yet been trodden; a thousand
salubrities and hidden islands of life. Unexhausted and undiscovered is still
man and man's world.   (*Philosophy of Nietzsche*, 448–9)

Then, these two aphoristic reflections of Roumain-Manuel evoke
the Nietzschean concept of *ewige Wiederkehr*, of "eternal return" (II,
1111:3):

La vie, c'est la vie: tu as beau prendre des chemins de traverse, faire un long
détour, la vie c'est un retour continuel.   (34)

Le fruit pourrit dans la terre et nourrit l'espoir de l'arbre nouveau.   (34)

Finally, the entire figure of Manuel – his "excès de vie," his lofty
aspirations, his larger-than-life utterances, reminds us of Nietzsche's
now overpopularized "Übermensch."

CONCLUSION

Let us return briefly to the form and ideational content of the aphorisms in *Gouverneurs de la rosée*. Although Roumain was demonstrably influenced by two dialectical thinkers in the (German)
"antagonistic" tradition, the sententious formulations in his last novel
clearly fall into the integrative, more straightforward category of
aphorisms typical of, say, Pascal. The ideational content of these
aphorisms complements and explains the narrative by proposing
collective solutions rooted in Marx, and human (or individual) remedial action reminiscent of Nietzsche.

6 *Pluie et vent sur Télumée Miracle*

Of the seven novels under consideration in this study, Simone Schwarz-Bart's *Pluie et vent* has generated the smallest amount of secondary literature. For example, no thoroughgoing analysis exists of the novel's lingual or narratological features. A recent introduction to five francophone Caribbean authors by Beverly Ormerod may contain the most complete piece of criticism published thus far on *Pluie et vent*. However, like the few other extant studies, it sets out mainly to summarize the plot, introduce characters, and detect recurring themes and motifs in the novel.

Further, nothing indicates that a clearly identifiable influence within the Western literary tradition has shaped Schwarz-Bart's work. Ormerod finds simply that Aimé Césaire, and in particular his *Cahier d'un retour au pays natal*, has served as a model for all Caribbean writers (1–16).

In the brief article on Schwarz-Bart in the Bordas *Dictionnaire de littératures de langue française* O. Biyidi rightly mentions, however, that the author's language is "nourrie de sentences" (2147). Her writing does not, however, appear to be informed by the French tradition of aphoristic writing, which lends a certain freshness to her text and makes a study of how she approaches aphorism particularly rewarding.

As regards Césaire and his possible influence on *Pluie et vent* – and, for that matter, on Caribbean literature generally – one of Ormerod's conclusions offers a fitting point of departure for a discussion of aphorisms and of the "equipment for living" they are likely to propose in this body of literature:

Each of these novels, then, projects a Césairean vision of the West Indian islands as "scars upon the water," flawed by an unjust social structure, inherited from the colonial era, which keeps the various sections of the community in a state of mutual estrangement and militates against the acceptance of racial or national identity. Many of the characters presented have little insight into the causes of their own alienation, and not all are fully aware of their situation as degrading or untenable; but even the most passive and resigned among them dream of escape from an impoverished and restrictive environment. (14)

The key idea in Ormerod's argument here is the "dream of escape from an impoverished and restrictive environment." If her assumption is correct, this "dream" is likely to find expression in the discourse of the characters in *Pluie et vent*.

THE NARRATOLOGICAL CONSEQUENCE OF APHORISM

We witness the aphorisms in *Pluie et vent* functioning on two broad levels. First, they explain the point of the narrative. On another level they convey "wisdom" through the speech of respected characters, as was the case in *Gouverneurs de la rosée*. Statistically, there are fewer aphoristic interventions in Schwarz-Bart's novel than in any of the other seven works under consideration. However, for the purposes of establishing a continuum, *Pluie et vent* should probably be inserted before the novels of Simon, Aquin, and Ramuz because of the prominence those interventions assume within the narrative.

Instead of following the Labovian pattern, in which evaluative elements follow the reported events, Schwarz-Bart often positions such devices so that they precede the actual narration. Thus, one often encounters an aphorism at the beginning of a segment of narrative. This unusual placement of a sentence that serves to explain the point of the story-line is reminiscent of some children's tales, or fables, in which the "moral" is stated from the outset rather than at the end of the narrative.

Accordingly, *Pluie et vent* begins with a fully formed aphorism. It emanates from the first-person narrative voice or, one could also argue, from an exterior, more anonymous voice: "Le pays dépend bien souvent du cœur de l'homme: il est minuscule si le cœur est petit, et immense si le cœur est grand" (11). "Cœur" is to be under-stood in its full semantic range, including the capacity to imagine, in this case, an improved situation.

The same technique is used a further ten times throughout the text, either at the commencement of a chapter or to inaugurate a narrative sequence (18, 23, 25, 46, 81, 109, 153, 166, 183).

It is worthy of note that the aphorisms in this category tend to display the hallmarks of written discourse – that is, the lexical choices, syntax, and rhythm are studied and polished. Contrary to the rest of the text, which suggests orality, these aphorisms convey a maximal concentration of thought expressed in the fewest possible words and in artfully balanced syntax. Moreover, these utterances contain no markers indicative of conversational "starting and stop-ping," nor do they contain the grammatical features typical of spon-taneous discourse. A brief look at two such excerpts from the novel will illustrate:

La vérité est qu'un rien, une idée, une lubie, un grain de poussière suffisent à changer le cours d'une vie.   (46)

La femme qui rit est celle-là même qui va pleurer, et c'est pourquoi on sait déjà, à la façon dont une femme est heureuse quel maintien elle aura devant l'adversité.   (153)

The next broad grouping of aphorisms in the novel results from the speech of those female characters (and, exceptionally, of one male character) who, through their lives and actions, command the reader's sympathy and respect. These stronger characters stand in contrast to the novel's defeated, shallow, or sadistic people, a notable example being Elie. This latter group seem incapable of formulating pithy words of wisdom.

One of the novel's key women is Télumée's grandmother, who redeems the entire narration from an underlying tone of despair. Ormerod says of her, "The images of resistance which provide con-tinuity throughout the many phases of Telumee's existence derive principally from the moral teaching of her grandmother" (119). That moral teaching of "Reine Sans Nom" is often delivered in terse, memorable sentences (see 40, 51, 77, 115, 132, 136, 137, 247) or, as Ormerod has already shown (119), in the form of allegory. At one point the grandmother fashions an allegory whose principal compo-nent is the archetypal figure of an untamed horse. She caps the story with an aphoristic injunction that is to become a leitmotiv in the novel: "Derrière une peine il y a une autre peine, la misère est une vague sans fin, mais le *cheval ne doit pas te conduire, c'est toi qui dois conduire le cheval*" (79, emphasis added).

Ormerod elaborates on this chiasmic aphorism, offering two valuable insights: "This tale is told to Télumée and Elie in their childhood; significantly, Elie runs home without waiting to hear the moral, which will come into question once more at the stormy end of his relationship with Télumée. The horse, the archetypal phallic animal, is an ancient symbol of unbridled human passion, and has widespread association with headlong catastrophe, darkness and death" (120). The grandmother's charge to Télumée ("Derrière une peine") features some elements of spoken discourse: second-person familiar verb markers and an impelling, almost spoken rhythm. Such characteristics are often found in orally transmitted proverbs. However, the chiasmus formed by the terms "cheval" and "tu/toi" are more features of written – that is, more carefully thought-out – discourse.

In addition to the bits of wisdom once spoken by Reine Sans Nom, Télumée also reveres two other persons, Amboise and Ismène. It is therefore not surprising that their sayings are repeatable. Schwarz-Bart confers a certain weight and dignity to those sayings, along with those of Reine Sans Nom, by casting them in condensed – that is, poetic or aphoristic – language. It is valuable to consider two such remarks. The first is attributed to Amboise, the second to Ismène:

Ami, rien ne poursuit le nègre que son propre cœur.   (147)

Voir tant de misères, recevoir tant de crachats, devenir impotent à mourir ... La vie sur terre convient-elle donc vraiment à l'homme?   (179)

With the reintroduction of the concepts of "grand cœur" (implied by "son propre cœur") and "petit cœur," ("impotent à mourir") both texts refer back to the aphorism that opens the entire book. One might thus speak of a coherent chain of aphorisms inserted at advisedly chosen points in the narrative.

INSIGHTS GAINED FROM A SEPARATE LISTING OF THE NOVEL'S APHORISMS

One of the building blocks that Schwarz-Bart chooses to construct her novel's aphorisms occurs throughout the whole of the text: She frequently employs a wide range of (metaphorical) images taken from nature: "un grain de poussière" (46), "une vague sans fin" (79), "l'océan" (81), "la foret" (109), "l'air, l'eau, le ciel et la terre" (115), "le soleil" (166), etc. These images serve as evidence to Beverley

Ormerod's more general statement that since Césaire, earthy images feature prominently in Caribbean novels (4–12).

With regard to the rhetorical composition of the book's aphoristic sentences, repetition might be seen as the most consistently observable text-building strategy. Deborah Tannen sheds light on the function and merit of repetition in discourse in general:

> Repeating a word, phrase or longer syntactic unit – exactly or with variation – results in a rhythmic pattern which sweeps the hearer or reader along. Simultaneously (as Derrida (1976) points out under the rubric of "iteration"), each time a word or phrase is repeated, its meaning is altered. The audience reinterprets the meaning of the word or phrase in light of the accretion, juxtaposition, or expansion; thus it participates in making meaning of the utterances. An extreme representation of this phenomenon is in Jerzy Kosinsky's novel *Being There*, in which a simple-minded gardener is thought brilliant by interlocutors whose words he repeats. The deep meaning which they glean from his utterances is their own work.   (576)

Akin to the device of repetition, one of the fundamental and recurrent themes of *Pluie et vent* is "eternal return." Accordingly, consider the way repetition in this representative aphorism serves to enact its semantic content: "On peut prendre *méandre* sur *méandre*, *tourner*, *contourner*, s'insinuer dans la terre, vos *méandres*, vous appartiennent mais la vie est là, patiente, sans commencement et sans fin, à vous attendre pareille à l'océan" (81, emphases mine). The image that rounds off the sentence, "l'océan," adds to the sense of repetition by evoking the action of incessant waves.

A number of analogous examples merit individual attention and analysis. In them, repetition may act to "sweep the hearer or reader along" or to displace discreetly a given word's original meaning – perhaps through tanaclasis. Witness, for example, the repetitious deployment of "cœur" (11), "il y a/il y aura" (25), "terre" (77), "grand" (79), "danser" (136), and "soleil" (166) as they function within their respective aphoristic propositions.

However, only in this one aspect, namely repetition as a rhetorical device, might one consider Schwarz-Bart's aphorisms to be "antagonistic" – that is, markedly response-provoking. Otherwise there emerge few structural traces in the novel's aphorisms of provocative irony or paradox. On the contrary, both the aphorisms and the work's other component parts generally use straightforward language and unambiguous referents. Thus, probably unwittingly, this francophone Caribbean novel perpetuates the integrative sententious tradition in literature instituted by the French *moralistes*.

One notable exception to this straightforwardness bears mentioning, however. A little over halfway through the novel the third-
person narrative voice joins with the group of oppressed women
featured in the narration to say: "Il faut stopper le mal par notre
silence et d'ailleurs, depuis quand la misère est-elle un conte?"
Through both a question and a sarcastic/ironic proposition, the
highly significant idea of attacking "la misère" by breaking the
silence and making a "conte" out of it is born. In this key sentence,
which is marked by the fact that it violates the relatively placid tone
of the other aphorisms, we might detect the quintessential "point" of
why this story is being told – namely, that only through breaking the
silence will a better situation be realized.

THE WORLD OF THE TEXT

Many of the book's aphorisms testify to the overall story-line's "celebration" of "the role of women in the Caribbean struggle for survival" (Ormerod 130), and of women generally. One might begin the
discussion with one obvious manifestation of this celebration. At
times Schwarz-Bart uses the conventional *homme* to signify "person"
or "humanity" in general (77, 166, 183). On many other occasions,
however, *femme* performs this generalizing function, and did so
before such usage was common:

La femme qui rit est celle-là même qui va pleurer, et c'est pourquoi on sait
déjà, à la façon dont une femme est heureuse quel maintien elle aura devant
l'adversité. (153)

Il me restait bien des découvertes à faire avant que je sache ce que signifie
exactement cela: *être une femme sur la terre*. (159, emphasis added)

In an altogether different thematic terrain within the novel, Ormerod detects the presence of a fundamental paradox in the text when
viewed in its entirety. Her concluding statement to the section of her
study that deals with *Pluie et vent* posits this idea: "Built upon the
paradoxical 'splendour of human uncertainty' (172) ['l'éclat du faste
de l'incertitude humaine' (248)], *The Bridge of Beyond* promises salvation through individual courage" (130). In light of Ormerod's observation, it is not surprising to encounter the two disparate strands of
incertitude and "salvation through individual courage" throughout
the text's "chain" of aphorisms.

On the one hand, we read of the beneficial consequences when "le
cœur est grand" (11) and of "riding the horse instead of being ridden

by it" (79). Reine Sans Nom, further, extols "un brave en équilibre sur une boule" (77) and in the same vein exhorts: "si grand que soit le mal, l'homme doit se faire encore plus grand, dut-il s'ajuster des échasses" (79).

On the other hand, however, the woman balancing on the ball "va tomber" (77). In conjunction with this event Reine Sans Nom enunciates a revision of one of the Beatitudes: "bienheureux celui qui navigue dans l'incertitude, qui ne sait ce qu'il a semé, ni ce qu'il va récolter" (132).

More pointedly, the usually silent Ismène almost cancels out the text's initial appeal for courage when, towards the close of the novel, she poses the rhetorical question: "voir tant de misères, recevoir tant de crachats, devenir impotent et mourir ... La vie sur terre convient-elle donc vraiment à l'homme?" (179)

CONCLUSION

Although Simone Schwarz-Bart deploys aphorism relatively infrequently in *Pluie et vent sur Télumée Miracle,* her placement of aphoristic sentences at the very beginning of the novel and *before* many of its narratological sequences causes them to assume marked prominence in the text. Further, most of the aphorisms emanate from a narrative voice vaguely foreign to any of the characters in the novel. That voice intervenes most often with unambiguous, forthright utterances reminiscent of the techniques generally used in French novels of the eighteenth century rather than in Caribbean spoken discourse.

These aphorisms, which form a logically flowing chain, contribute significantly to the novel's coherence. In following their "movement," we notice that they help the reader to discern Schwarz-Bart's model of human existence. The first sentence of the novel, an aphorism, inaugurates the work on an optimistic note. Progressively, ever more insurmountable complications to the simple formula of "[le pays] est minuscule si le cœur est petit, et immense si le cœur est grand" are introduced. After this bulk of precariousness, the novel closes not with an affirmation but with a question mark that is reflected in several aphoristic formulations: "la vie sur terre convient-elle vraiment à l'homme?" (179) and "la vie est une mer sans escale, sans phare aucun, ... et les hommes sont des navires sans destination" (247–8).

The progression of thought conveyed by these aphorisms – and by the thought and action of the various women and men portrayed in the novel – might best be regarded as cyclical rather than linear: an eternal round of initial innocence and optimism, then harsh experience, and later the recognition that life is "sans escale" and must be confronted "sans phare aucun" (247). None the less, a degree of the initial optimism is retained in the very fact that the woman narrator lives to tell her story and to pass on the wisdom – often in the form of aphoristic sentences – that she has so painfully acquired. Through the act of story-telling, inscribing the story, then commenting on it, a step is taken towards making the dream of "escape" and betterment closer to becoming a reality.

7 *La Route des Flandres*

The all too brief pages allotted here to Claude Simon's best-known work will run counter to the critical mainstream, which posits the impracticability of establishing meaning from this novel's narrative sequences. J.A.E. Loubère offers a tidy summary of the prevailing view of the secondary literature: "Far from bringing elucidation, the text [Simon] elaborates refuses to resolve itself in information. It demonstrates instead that it is the enemy of information, either because of its power to breed new texts ... or because of its tendency to peter out and vanish in the deserts of the imagination" (102). Immediately following this statement, Loubère raises another challenging point: "We are left, then, with the narrative itself. Clearly, the 'meaning' of the narration lies only in its own constitution" (102).

Indeed, the study of this novel's narrative structure, a topic largely neglected in the critical literature, turns out to be particularly productive. Previous studies of the novel have leaned towards plot summary (Kadish), analysis of its characterizations (Loubère and Kadish), and discussion of the text's pervasive eroticism (Kadish and Jiménez).

Loubère is again particularly useful when, in exceptionally succinct language, he discerns the fundamental substance of the novel. While challenging the traditional critical move of establishing a narrative "point of view" in the case of *La route des Flandres*, he raises still another issue:

What is there in the mind, which allows, invents, or presupposes any particular point of view? Is there not simply a tangle of memories, a forest of perceptions, a world of fantasies stimulated by the senses and the word, forming a whole forever complete and forever changing? How can this chaotic, undefined mass be reconciled with itself, or with similar "magma" (as Simon calls it) in the minds of others? George ends by confessing that he cannot *know*, that he has perhaps invented the whole story of Iglésia and Corinne. But in that case, what of the story and history, what of certainty and the belief that in the life of each and every one of us something has happened?   (103–4)

In light of such an elusive narrative, which questions the very validity of recounting events that occurred in the past, it is with some hesitation that one ventures a study of "aphorism" or aphoristic formulation within that narrative. Further, one would think that a text that seeks to represent the "magma," "forever complete and forever changing," that characterizes a human consciousness would most probably avoid inscribing aphoristic formulations.

To complicate the matter further, Loubère rightly goes on to caution about studies of the novel that use the cut-and-paste technique: "The result [in *La Route des Flandres*] is a narrative of such coherence and power that any attempt to separate the interwoven images from one another is an act of mutilation" (102).

It is nonetheless a fruitful exercise to become aware of the various categories of "images" that comprise the narrative. Such an awareness might prevent a too-hasty dismissal of the text, especially on the part of the uninitiated student. Two broad questions emerge as we approach the text in the context of aphoristic discourse within the novel: How might *La Route des Flandres* transcend being simply "a chaotic and undefined mass?" and how do the various images in question combine in order to produce the "coherence and power" Loubère perceives in the work?

Once we have attempted to come to grips with the novel through focused consideration of its narrative components, and after weighing the critical "consensus" on its supposed indeterminacy, we might become intrigued by the following, at first glance impressionistic, comment by Lucien Dällenbach:

Mais à supposer que [le lecteur] ait la curiosité et la bonne volonté nécessaire pour souscrire au "contrat de lecture" que nous avons évoqué, quelles sont les difficultés qui l'attendent?

Pour en donner une idée sans tomber dans les travers démagogiques et pseudo-pédagogiques d'un *Simon mode d'emploi* ou un *Simon sans peine*, il faut effectuer un retour au texte, *méditer les passages où il se met en abyme*, examiner les conditions qu'il pose à son intellection et, surtout, repérer les cheminements et les opérations mentales auxquels il contraint son destinataire. (34, emphasis added)

Although Dällenbach rather surprisingly (for a contemporary critic) suggests a "mise en abyme" of the author himself, and further advises the reader to meditate on the corresponding passages in the text, he in fact does not stray far from the post-structuralist critics. In a relevant endnote he asserts that Simon avoids the "grande indélicatesse" of consciously inserting "theories" into his texts. Instead, in Dällenbach's view, "les passages réflexifs ne se distinguent pas scripturalement des autres, d'où le plus souvent une réflexivité *ad libitum*" (201).

Quoting Dällenbach in this context is not to imply that *La Route des Flandres* can be interpreted or that definitive "meaning" can be attributed to the text. It can simply be argued that there are certain "points" to the story, certain reasons for its being told, to evoke William Labov.

In the novel the operations of the "magma"/consciousness (among many other phenomena) are working to reconstruct – albeit in a highly fragmentary fashion – a story. The reader observes these operations through the medium of a written text. In conventional, Proustian fashion, past events are being recalled/reconstructed/reported by use of past-tense verb markers. Far more difficult to analyse is the development of an ostensibly chaotic web of "réflexivité."

This being so, how might the reader become aware of and approach the narrator's "evaluations" as the various events are being recounted? First, many of the reflective, highly concentrated passages in the work far surpass the banality of the quotidian and are eminently worthy of an effort to make sense of them. Next, it can be demonstrated that within *La Route des Flandres* the results of the narrator's reflective consciousness are often cast in particularly terse, universalizing linguistic structures. As Dällenbach suggests, a "powerful" reading experience can be derived from making the effort to recognize and "meditate" on such formulations. Additionally, we must continually ask how the reflective portions of the text relate to the narration in order to produce a rewarding experience.

THE NARRATOLOGICAL CONSEQUENCE OF APHORISM

The novel opens with a series of sequentially ordered, unproblematic narrative clauses that report past events: "Il [Captain Reixach, we

find out later] tenait une lettre à la main, il leva les yeux, me regarda
... je pouvais voir aller et venir passer les taches rouges acajou ocre
des chevaux qu'on menait à l'abreuvoir" (9). The work closes with a
coda-like re-evocation of these opening events. As was the case in
the novel's opening lines, Simon uses the preterit/imperfect to
"report" them: "Mais peut-être doutait-il [de Reixach] encore qu'elle
... lui fût infidèle peut-être fut-ce seulement en arrivant qu'il trouva
quelque chose comme une preuve, quelque chose qui le décida"
(294), and "feignant [de Reixach] toujours de ne rien voir pensif et
futile sur ce cheval tandis qu'il s'avançait à la rencontre de sa mort
dont le doigt était déjà posé" (295). These same events are reported
again and again throughout the novel, each time in varied permutations and juxtaposed against new combinations of supplementary
material.

The two foregoing passages, which frame the novel, are featured
together here in order to sensitize the reader to similar ones throughout the entire work in which events are reported using the conventional past tenses. The reader can rely on such clauses with preterite/
imperfect verbs in order to lay out the puzzle pieces of the narration
and, if desired, to rearrange them mentally into some kind of mean-
ingful sequence.

It must be emphasized, however, that exponents of the *nouveau
roman* break away from a conventional, temporal ordering of events
by design, and that they eschew facile plots designed to please or to
entertain. In view of the difficulties presented by such fragmented
narrations, when the narrators of *nouveaux romans* break away from
a bare recounting of events to inject evaluative material, such backgrounded clauses become perhaps even more crucial in the process
of sense-making than they are in conventional, linear narrations.

The two passages that follow are excerpted from the middle section
of the novel in order to illustrate this contention further. A short piece
of event-recounting, cast in the preterit/imperfect, is retained in each
case as a reminder of the contrast between the two general categories
of "reporting" versus "evaluation" suggested by Labov:

Blum possédait héréditairement une connaissance (l'intelligence avait dit
Georges, mais pas seulement cela: plus encore: *l'expérience intime, atavique,
passée au stade du réflexe, de la stupidité et de la méchanceté humaines*).   (159,
emphasis added)

Blum se fit porter malade et rentra lui aussi au camp, et ils y restèrent tous
les deux ... tandis qu'ils essayaient de se transporter par procuration (c'est-
à-dire au moyen de leur imagination, c'est-à-dire en rassemblant et combinant

tout ce qu'ils pouvaient trouver dans leur mémoire en fait de connaissances vues ou lues … de façon … à faire surgir … *l'innommable réalité dans cet univers futile, mystérieux et violent.*   (173, emphasis added)

As these two passages demonstrate, when evaluation of the narrative is presented, the narrator of the novel suspends the normal flow of reporting, only more imperceptibly than in traditional texts. The evaluative material is often none the less marked. Suspension of the narrative flow can be signalled either metalingually (the parentheses or the colon might correspond to a pause and a change in intonation) or lexically by such locutions as *c'est-à-dire, il me semblait,* or *sans doute.* These devices are borrowings and adaptations from spoken, as opposed to written, discourse.

Also, as can be noted from the two excerpts above, the evaluated material often contains devices more common to written discourse than to spontaneous thought or speech. In each of the cases above a sophisticated gradation is formed by the careful ordering of three advisedly selected terms.

Labov and Hopper conclude that evaluative or backgrounded clauses are also marked grammatically. If we adhere to their schematics, Simon often conforms to the usual pattern of constructing "reflective" fragments with verbs in the durative or iterative present tense (see Appendix E: 12, 18, 19, etc.). More frequently, however, the text's "reflexivity" is cast in elliptical, parenthetical interjections containing no verb at all. Salvador Jiménez, in the *Twayne* study on Simon, detects the presence of such "parenthetical" interpolations but does not analyse how they function (68).

It is also striking how often Simon deploys the demonstrative adjective (ce/cette/ces), not only in its ordinary role of pointing towards an object within one's range of perception but instead to posit universals of experience. The technique may also be seen to coax a degree of complicity out of the reader, something in the vein of "you know that …" The reader might either quickly agree, if the proposed object or action is also a part of his/her experience, or instead begin to examine the proposition critically. One representative example of this unique phenomenon bears close reading and analysis. The narrator (Georges?) is recounting events in which he himself had supposedly taken part: "Il remontait la pente de la colline, … il redescendait la pente, tournait encore, longeait le bas de la colline, puis se précipitait, se ruait de nouveau … Georges savait alors qu'il allait peu à peu le voir apparaître, s'élevant, se hissant" (32). At this point, with no transitional device other than the preposition "avec," the text abandons the simple reporting of events and posits a universal we are supposed to recognize, or at least relate to in some way: "avec cette irrésistible lenteur de tout ce qui de près ou de loin et de quelque espèce que ce soit – hommes, animaux, mécaniques – touche aux choses de la terre" (32).

We also sense traces typical of aphoristic formulation: "definition" ("lenteur/choses de la terre") and provocative hyperbole ("*tout* ce qui de près ou de loin et de quelque espèce que ce soit"). Some form of hyperbole is present in many of the great quantity of aphoristic fragments that commence, similarly, with a demonstrative adjective (34–5, 43, 70, 83–4, 114, 115, 120, 162, 166, 173, 231, 286, 289).

In conclusion, we are confronted with a highly unconventional textual layout intended to mirror the workings of a consciousness: with erratic punctuation or a near absence of it, with the starts, stops, and "repairing" common to spontaneous discourse, and a highly fluid topicality. As Dällenbach pointed out, such a "chaotic" text makes the "reflective" (evaluative) passages difficult to distinguish from the reconstruction of past events. Indeed, in the workings of the consciousness, they are perhaps only distinguishable in hindsight.

These two narrative operations are in turn difficult to distinguish from the narrator's perception and recording of other phenomena taking place concurrently – that is, in the present. Despite all the apparent chaos, however, the disparate elements do combine to form a coherent – even if not totally decipherable – entity.

INSIGHTS GAINED FROM A SEPARATE LISTING OF THE NOVEL'S APHORISMS

The controversial argument that Simon "se met en abyme" in his text might be supported by several of the aphorisms in *La Route des Flandres*. Two of them particularly serve to evidence this hypothesis.

Georges, the principal character in the narration, endeavours incessantly to "know" for certain how Reixach died. Abruptly sandwiched between two opposing theories about his former captain's weapon, there appears a fully formed aphorism on the ostensibly incongruous topic of reading novels. A change in frames is subtly indicated by the abrupt use of a capital letter. The period and double space normally used to close off a sentence are absent. The aphorism in question reads: "Les gens aiment tellement faire de la tragédie du drame du roman" (262). We know Georges to concern himself only casually with writing, documentation, and historiography; so from where does this rather surprising, discreetly sarcastic reflection about "people's" drive to transform a novel's "drama" into a tragedy emanate? Such a thought seems better to represent the critical sensibilities of

the "new" novelist, Simon, than those of Georges, the main character/
narrator in the text.

At another point in the novel a more anonymous, third-person
narrator recounts events in which Blum and Georges were involved.
This voice uses the most banal of sensations, hunger, as a pretext to
explore modes of perceiving reality: "Et tous les deux (Georges et
Blum) assis les jambes pendantes sur le rebord de leur couchette, en
train d'essayer de se figurer qu'ils n'avaient pas faim (ce qui était
assez facile, parce *qu'un homme peut arriver à se faire croire à peu près
n'importe quoi pourvu que ça l'arrange*: mais beaucoup plus difficile, et
même impossible, d'en persuader aussi le rat qui, sans repos, leur
dévorait le ventre" (112, emphasis added). Here again the aphoristic
reflection seems to be interpolated into the text by a mind defter at
articulating finely discriminating philosophical investigations than
are the minds of any of the novel's characters.

Another curiosity in the novel results from those exceptional utterances that have been endowed with relatively sophisticated rhetorical
devices. One must ask where a chiasmic formulation such as the following is generated: "cet attachement hautain du maître pour son
chien et de bas en haut du chien pour son maître" (43). Is it constructed
spontaneously by an ever-fluid, chaotic magma/consciousness or by
a professional writer used to contriving, revising, and honing?

Then what of this finely constructed gradation: "cette fausse *insouciance*, cette fausse *gaieté*, ce faux *cynisme* des jeunes gens" (120)? Does
it result from deliberate thought and polish – from the author's craft
– or from the spontaneous, randomly operating consciousness of a
person engaged in workaday activity and thought?

The well-written, highly "literary" sentences cited above, however,
do not typify the bulk of the novel's aphoristic reflections. Most of
them contain ambiguities and imperfections that detract from their
ability to clarify, to convey "information," or to stimulate the reader's
consciousness through easily recognizable rhetorical means. Often
they are constructed with curious interrogative locutions that with
subtlety call something into question: for example, "ce comment
s'appelait-il philosophe" (33), "à moins que, justement, ... ce soit
cela:" (48), "sans doute" (70), or "comment peut-on dire" (99). Such
"investigations" are sometimes accompanied by a question mark,
sometimes not. They provoke the reader into becoming involved –
as if in conversation with someone – and into formulating his or her
own opinion on the topic at hand. (See also the aphorisms found on
pages 95, 111, 123, 161, 285, 285, 289, etc.)

Sometimes such exploratory utterances are combined with an
attempt to define. In these cases any hope of obtaining reliable

information – for instance, about love – is indeed shattered: "À moins que, justement, l'amour – ou plutôt la passion – ce soit cela: cette chose muette, ces élans, ces répulsions, ces haines, tout informulé – et même informé, et donc cette simple suite de gestes, de paroles de scènes insignifiantes, et, au centre, sans préambule, cet assaut, ce corps-à-corps urgent, rapide sauvage n'importe où" (48–9).

Another feature of this novel's aphoristic formulations is their frequent reliance on superlatives. Fricke placed this device at the head of his enumeration, probably because of its frequent incidence. Propositions that contain overstated elements, we recall, tend to cause the reader to compare them with his or her own experience. The chaotic magma/consciousness Simon presents to us in *La Route des Flandres* abounds with subtle overreactions. Cases such as the following (with emphasis added in each case) account for a major part of the "power" the text possesses to involve and challenge the reader: "le *pire* des abandons" (12); "il est *inévitable*" (18); "comme *toute* mascarade" (75); "*seulement* les hommes" (162); "cette *totale* absence de sens moral" (166), etc.

A comment on those aphorisms that share common topics needs to be made. Although the aphoristic fragments I have lifted from the text might stand alone eminently well and make sense without any surrounding context, allowing them to take on such independence constitutes a deformation of Claude Simon's text. If *La Route des Flandres* represents an ongoing exploration or, in Loubère's words, "a whole forever complete and forever changing," then the repetition of a given topic from aphorism to aphorism will, of necessity, continually displace signification. Such a transformation of previous meaning occurs both through the internal construction of the aphoristic fragment and through its appearance in ever-differing narrative contexts.

To illustrate how this phenomenon works, we might follow through the topic of "time" each time it is treated within the novel's concentrated "reflective" sentence fragments (19, 28, 52, 99, 231, 296). It would be necessary to ascertain what has been added and subtracted from the inaugural "le temps n'existe pas" (19) and how the surrounding elements of the narrative influence each appearance of the topic. In the final analysis, it would be impossible to draw any conclusions, either from any one of the aphorisms or from all of them together. Rather, we are confronted with an open-ended exploration whose details are often contradictory and tend to cancel each other out.

To summarize, Simon's aphoristic propositions, considered both individually and in "chains" within the whole of the novel, break clearly from the mould of the "integrative" French moralists; rather,

Simon presents provocative inquiries that defy closure on a wide range of topics. None the less, a degree of meaning can be established, especially from the aphoristic fragments. It is only that the meaning is volatile.

THE WORLD OF THE TEXT

With the four previous novels, perusing a separate listing of the text's aphoristic formulations often serves to confirm insights already brought to light in the critical literature. To a certain extent the same holds true in the case of *La Route des Flandres*. The major studies have pointed out, for instance, the novel's preoccupation with love and love-making (see 48–9, 52, 111, 115), with time and movement (19, 28, 52, 99, 231, 296), with a mistrust for traditional epistemology and the written word (34–5, 56, 95, 111, 112, 123, 162, 173, 282, 285, 289), with the ephemeral nature of reality and man's perception of it (95, 99, 123, 161, 173, 285, 296), with war, violence, and destruction (18, 33–4, 70, 83–4, 282, 296).

Of perhaps new interest, however, is the overall "world" the novel projects and the possible "equipment for living" it might suggest. Both emerge from less evident themes that become apparent as we consider the novel's aphoristic formulations.

A particularly interesting reflection, which uses the unusual comparison of a typhoon, appears during the narrator's (anti)solution to the enigma of Reixach's death. It turns out that in order to "solve" the enigma, two disparate sets of knowledge would have to be merged. This proves impossible, however. The point of tangency between the two bodies of knowledge – or between two separate seats of consciousness – represents a kind of virgin territory for Simon: "Cette espèce de néant comme on dit qu'au centre d'un typhon il existe une zone parfaitement calme de la connaissance, de point zéro" (296). Simon's formulation, "point zéro," recalls Roland Barthes's well-known hypothesis of a "degré zéro de l'écriture" – a totally innocent, completely self-referential kind of writing. Barthes's influence on Simon may be possible in this instance, for Barthes had published his set of essays not long (seven years) before the appearance of *La Route des Flandres*.

One may go so far as to speak of an almost metaphysical drive in Simon's novel towards some kind of inviolable paradise, towards a complete "néant" or "disparition de toute idée de tout concept" (285). (See also 52, 67, 114, 166, 282, 296.)

Although it would be reckless to refer to *La Route des Flandres* as an ideological novel, rather surprisingly one encounters in the text not infrequent commentary on Marxism as a teleological ethos. The lengthy fragment that follows reflects succinctly the core of the "historical process" as elaborated by Marx. However, far from proclaiming the virtues of Marxism, through the agency of the locution "l'un comme l'autre" Simon seems instead to point out that there can be no "progress" towards the desired final cause:

Ce comment s'appelait-il philosophe qui a dit que l'homme ne connaissait que deux moyens de s'approprier ce qui appartient aux autres, la guerre et le commerce, et qu'il choisissait en général tout d'abord le premier parce qu'il lui paraissait le plus facile et le plus rapide et ensuite, mais seulement après avoir découvert les inconvénients et les dangers du premier, le second, c'est-à-dire le commerce qui était un moyen non moins déloyal et brutal mais plus confortable, et qu'au demeurant tous les peuples étaient obligatoirement passés par ces deux phases et avaient chacun à son tour mis l'Europe à feu et à sang avant de se transformer en sociétés anonymes de commis-voyageur comme les Anglais mais que guerre et commerce n'étaient jamais l'un comme l'autre que l'expression de leur rapacité elle-même la conséquence de l'ancestrale terreur de la faim et de la mort, ce qui faisait que tuer voler piller et vendre n'étaient en réalité qu'une seule et même chose un simple besoin celui de se rassurer, comme des gamins qui sifflent et chantent fort pour se donner du courage en traversant une forêt la nuit.   (33–4)

The following aphoristic reflections likewise evoke the Marxian paradigm of class struggle. The universalizing demonstrative pronoun in the first quotation and the idea of "pratiquement impossible à lever" in the second likewise betray Simon's lack of confidence in the possibility of changing inequality through belief in and adherence to a teleological system:

Cet attachement hautain du maître pour son chien et de bas en haut du chien pour son maître.   (43)

Cette hypothèque pratiquement impossible à lever que constitue entre deux êtres humains une énorme différence de disponibilités monétaires, puis de grades.   (287)

Yet Simon seems to adhere to a fundamentally Marxist conception of literature, in so far as it critiques traditional modes of writing and reading. Consider, in this connection, a remarkable bit of commentary akin to the Sartrian concept of "bourgeois" literature: "comme ça doit être chouette d'avoir tellement de temps à sa disposition que le suicide, le drame, la tragédie deviennent des sortes d'élégants passe-temps" (268). With an extreme economy of words, Simon likewise seems to be mocking "cet impérieux souci d'élégance" (286) in artistic, and particularly literary creation.

In conjunction with the "historical process," the remarks in the novel on atavistically determined, unexamined "reflexes," especially those that prove destructive or inhumane, are strikingly derogatory. One example will suffice here, but the reader is referred to complementary aphoristic fragments found on pages 18, 111, and 161: "l'expérience intime, atavique, passée au stade du réflexe, de la stupidité et de la méchanceté humaines" (159).

Finally, the novel bristles, not only in its reflective or aphoristic passages but also throughout the entire narrative, with representations of keen modes of perception and memory. One recalls as one rereads Simon the analogous, seminal endeavour of Proust in *A la recherche du temps perdu*. Witness, to begin, this idiosyncratic redefinition of "involuntary memory," expressed this time conversely, namely as an *inability to forget*: "Il y a des choses que le pire des abandons des renoncements ne peut faire oublier même si on le voulait et ce sont en général les plus absurdes les plus vides de sens celles qui ne se raisonnent ni se commandent" (12).

Few authors have ventured a hypothetical description of one's perceptions at the moment of a violent and sudden death. The leap from a rather banal observation, here of a facial expression, to philosophical "reflection" is effected through the ever-present comparator "comme/comme si":

cet air un peu niais, surpris, incrédule et doux qu'ont ceux des gens tués de mort violente, comme si au dernier moment leur avait été révélé quelque chose à quoi durant toute leur vie ils n'avaient jamais eu l'idée de penser, c'est-à-dire sans doute quelque chose d'absolument contraire à ce que peut apprendre la pensée, de tellement étonnant, de tellement.   (70)

There follows in the novel a nuanced addition to the age-old discussion on the delineation between "spirit" and "body":

le point critique où l'esprit (pas le corps, qui peut en supporter beaucoup plus) ne peut plus endurer une minute de plus l'idée – le supplice – de posséder quelque chose qui peut être mangé.   (71)

In the succeeding passage the narrator attributes thought to one of the other characters, Iglésia. In the tradition of Baudelaire, the symbolists, and the phenomenologists Simon revisits the subject's capacity to establish correspondences between people, abstract concepts, and objects in nature:

ces objets parmi lesquels il rangeait sans doute les vedettes de cinéma (privées de toute réalité, sauf féerique), les chevaux, ou encore ces choses (montagnes, bateaux, avions, auxquelles l'homme qui perçoit par leur intermédiaire les manifestations des forces naturelles contre lesquelles il lutte, attribue des réactions (colère, méchanceté, traîtrise) humaines: êtres (les chevaux, les déesses sur celluloïd, les autos) d'une nature hybride, ambiguë, pas tout à fait humains, pas tout à fait objets, inspirant à la fois le respect et l'irrespect par la rencontre, la réunion en eux d'éléments composants (réels ou supposés) disparates – humains et inhumains.   (132–3)

CONCLUSION

Out of this disparate array of threads there emerges something of a common strand, made manifest by a close – and yet global – reading of all this novel's highly condensed fragments of reflective, universalizing thought.

The characters, and particularly their aphoristic reflections, exhibit a preoccupation with "un simple besoin, celui de se rassurer" (33–4, 112). A host of more detailed but related concerns contribute to this general one: the desire for "attachement" (43), "communication," and "compréhension" (56–7, also 48–9). Related to this desire is what Simon terms a "superstitieuse crédulité" in language, in invented images conveyed lingually – especially by the written word. Simon seems to be arguing that humanity believes that language can somehow fulfil the quest for solidity and permanence (34–5, 56–7, 67, 173, 268, 286). Finally, fused to the concepts of the desire for comprehension/love and the illusory nature of language is the drive to "know," to obtain the "certitude" of this or that reality (123, 285).

Nothing in Simon's text indicates that these needs and desires can be satisfied. What remains, the only thing that is certain in this text, clearly negates our received – that is, humanist or Marxian – ideals concerning union, understanding, and the transmission of knowledge.

With ease Simon reduces love to "ce corps-à-corps urgent," to "passion … cette chose muette, ces élans, ces répulsions, ces haines" (48–9). For Simon, no evidence suggests that humanity has, or ever will, overcome "cette hypothèque … que constitue entre deux êtres humains une énorme différence de disponibilité monétaires, puis de grades" (287, also 43). In this text Western civilization has merely "progressed" from being "à feu et à sang" to an analogous state of "sociétés anonymes de commis-voyageur." Both solutions, in Simon's eyes, represent no more than "l'expression de leur rapacité elle-même la conséquence de l'ancestrale terreur de la faim et de la mort, ce qui faisait que tuer voler piller et vendre n'étaient en réalité qu'une seule et même chose" (33-4).

In the "world" projected by *La Route des Flandres* humanity constitutes little more than an assemblage of "gens stupides et sans éducation" (18), "des ambitions, des rêves, des vanités, des futiles et impérissables passions" (52, also 71, 99, 115), of "la stupidité et ... la méchanceté humaines" (159, also 132-3). Movement itself ("le temps de parcourir à son tour une dizaine ou une quinzaine de mètres") proves "futile and illusory" (231).

As regards venerated epistemological systems and their collusion with language, in the words of Simon, "[le] savoir appris par procuration" and "ce qui est écrit" (34-5) – these too can be unmasked as merely the "inflexible perfidie des choses créées ou asservies par l'homme, [qui] se retournent contre lui et se vengent avec d'autant plus de traîtrise et d'efficacité qu'elles semblent docilement remplir leur fonction" (56-7). In sum, the only things of which one can be sure are immediate appetites and death. That Simon would choose the vulgar *bouffer* and *crever* to express this idea seems less than innocent, for the words hint at a flippantly cynical, perhaps even bitter attitude: "à part la certitude de crever qu'est-ce qu'il y a de plus réel? ... la certitude qu'il faut bouffer" (123).

The novel does, however, offer another "solution" to the desire for union, understanding, and reassurance. At the extreme opposite of corruption, futile passions, the ravages of time, and the treachery of language, Simon posits virginity (67, 114), immobility (67), inviolability (67), a total "absence de sens moral ou de charité dont sont seulement capables les enfants" (166), nothingness, a "point zéro" (296).

The world projected by Simon's text proves remarkable, for if there is any middle ground between the two opposite poles of corruption and virginity, such an arrangement remains only implied in *La Route des Flandres*. No evidence can be found in the text of any acts that would attenuate or explain the pervasive violence and egotistical satisfaction of passions. However, there is an equally pervasive preoccupation with starting over again from scratch, with an inviolable existence that is free from corruption. In this novel the search for meaning and truth collapses, and its movements are "atomized" – that is, scattered into still further permutations, these as ephemeral and elusive as their precedents (285, 296).

As for an "equipment for living," this text goes past the notion of absurdity proposed, say, by Camus in *Le Mythe de Sisyphe*. Indeed, Simon proposes no philosophical reason at all for living – or for choosing suicide – as did the existentialists. The only "remedy" to a civilization past redemption is a clear slate. But as is indicated by the final (aphoristic) lines of the book, even the results of a clear slate will probably end up disintegrating "peu à peu par morceaux comme une bâtisse abandonnée." Any brave new world will itself eventually prove "inutilisable" and be delivered over to "l'incohérent, nonchalant, impersonnel et destructeur travail du temps."

8 *Présence de la mort*

EXTRATEXTUAL CONSIDERATIONS

In one of the more recent overviews of Ramuz's work David Bevan devotes only a single line to *Présence de la mort* (59). Instead, he turns his attention to three novels of the author's mature period: *La Grande Peur dans la montagne* (1926), *Farinet ou la fausse monnaie* (1932), and *Derborence* (1934). Bevan and many other critics consider these later works to be Ramuz's finest.

Philippe Renaud implicitly challenges this prevalent view – that is, that Ramuz's writing of the early and middle period is somehow inferior – when he writes in the preface to the 1978 republication of *Présence de la mort* (1922): "Chef-d'œuvre méconnu, *Présence de la mort* n'est pas un Ramuz parmi d'autres: c'est le grand rassemblement de ses œuvres antérieures; son univers, comme la terre au premier chapitre, revient à son origine "pour s'y refondre," et de ce creuset émergent les figures de livres à venir. Ce texte unique pourrait s'intituler *Toute-présence de Ramuz*" (1).

To be sure, all Ramuz's major concerns appear in *Présence de la mort*, making it a fitting representative of his entire corpus. Also, for the purposes of this study *Présence de la mort* offers a significant number of aphorisms; the later works, by contrast, progressively renounce aphoristic intervention. For example, the mature work *Derborence* contains not a single fully formed aphorism and only very little aphoristic language.

Ramuz's steady tendency away from editorial commentary, at least in his texts of imaginative prose, should not come as a surprise.

Within the pivotal *Présence de la mort* the narrator, simultaneously recounting the novel's catastrophic events and "dip[ping] his pen into the ink," utters this suggestion to himself: "Regarder ce qui est, et rien mettre ici que ce qui est" (34).

Some eight years earlier Ramuz had consolidated his ideas on literary creation into a kind of credo-manifesto: *L'Exemple de Cézanne*. In this brief essay he enunciates this same philosophy of writing, which becomes more refined with the writing of each novel. One of Cézanne's tenets, which he himself had cast into an aphorism (which Ramuz reproduces verbatim in the essay), expresses the essence of Ramuz's *L'Exemple de Cézanne*: "Peindre d'après nature, ce n'est pas copier l'objectif, c'est réaliser des sensations" (26). Ramuz, too, would endeavour to re-present "nature" (defined here as "ce qui est") and not to "copy" it; rather, he would seek to re-present judiciously chosen elements from nature in order to "bring about sensations." It follows that aphoristic editorializing would find little place amid words whose principal aim it is to create sensations on the part of the text-recipient.

Such an enterprise, of course, might easily be confused with the project of the "new novelists." One might best differentiate the two approaches by contrasting the typically Ramuzian penchant for "gaucherie" with the smooth, hyper-real, cinematographic images of the "new novel."

To illustrate further, in a different kind of tribute to Cézanne, Ramuz wrote: "Cézanne peint devant la nature à peu près comme on assemble les morceaux d'un jeu de patience devant un modèle à reproduire. Les toiles sont une juxtaposition de taches colorées, où jamais le dessin linéaire ne paraît. Mais la science des masses et des valeurs est si sûre, sous son apparence de gaucherie, qu'il n'a pas besoin de cette aide. Cézanne ne copie pas, il transpose" (*Exemple*, 45–6).

Important to retain from this discussion of Ramuz's method is his aim to inscribe ostensibly awkward juxtapositions of "taches colorées" while writing into the text the least possible amount of commentary, or "evaluation." He achieves the desired result to such an advanced degree in, for instance, *Derborence*, that an uninitiated reading of the work can prove baffling. However, if we approach the text with a basic foreknowledge of Ramuz's world of ideas and his conception of artistic creation, we are struck by how the seemingly primitive images, juxtaposed in "crude" fashion, "create sensations" and thereby offer a highly idiosyncratic, subject-oriented reading experience.

Returning to the concept of aphorism as it relates to Ramuz's corpus, it must have proven difficult for him to resist including tidy "evaluative" sentences in his works of fiction. Indeed, his earlier

imaginative prose and all his essays abound with terse, even sententious propositions. This one from the well-known essay "Taille de
l'homme" might be singled out, for it neatly demonstrates Ramuz's
facility with the genre. Further, it gets quickly to the heart of his
paradoxical (anti)metaphysics, as expressed particularly in *Présence
de la mort*:

La grandeur est-elle matérielle ou spirituelle, ou les deux choses séparément,
ou les deux choses à la fois?

On se rappelle le mot de Pascal: "Quand l'univers l'écraserait, l'homme
serait encore plus noble que ce qui le tue, parce qu'il sait qu'il meurt; et
l'avantage que l'univers a sur lui, l'univers n'en sait rien." L'homme sait,
c'est sa grandeur, mais la grandeur n'existe que si elle est constatée, et
constatée par quelqu'un. Y a-t-il donc quelqu'un hors de l'homme pour la
constater? *Car l'homme passe et ses œuvres passent: c'est même la seule chose dont
l'homme soit sûr.*   (191–2, emphasis added)

THE NARRATOLOGICAL CONSEQUENCE
OF APHORISM

Given Ramuz's endeavour to produce sensations mainly through
visual imagery, it is not surprising that only a few passages in
Présence de la mort contain fully formed aphorisms. Even fewer
intrude into the text, having been conspicuously placed there by an
extraneous omniscient narrator. For example, Ramuz puts himself
exceptionally "en abyme" when he introduces the novel with "On
n'a pas beaucoup d'imagination chez nous" (16).

Likewise, the three bits of relatively blatant commentary that follow, excerpted from later sections of the text, contrast sharply with
the other elements of the narration and with the style generally:

Il faudrait pouvoir imaginer le ciel, les astres, les continents, les océans,
l'équateur, les deux pôles. Or, on n'imagine rien que soi et ce qui est autour
de soi.   (18)

Les choses qu'on devra quitter, peut-être … les aimer davantage. Et connaître
enfin l'espace, le généreux, le varié le large et long, l'abondant, le très vaste,
– dans sa solitude et sa nudité.   (24)

Un homme comme ça, c'est-à-dire comme beaucoup d'autres, multipliant,
additionnant, faisant des soustractions.   (28)

All these aphoristic comments correspond to the thought of Ramuz,
clearly and directly expressed in his essays and journals.

Later in the text we are probably also reading Ramuz the essayist when he interrupts the reporting of the people's first reactions to the inexplicable rise in temperature: "La plupart des hommes sont ainsi faits qu'ils ne peuvent s'intéresser qu'à l'immédiat et au détail; ils aiment à se laisser tromper. Peu lèvent les yeux jusqu'au ciel, peu le comprennent. Peu savent même qu'il existe, et là-haut le grand mécanisme, l'astre plus ou moins proche, l'astre se rapprochant toujours" (48).

When we use William Labov's schematics to analyse the text's narrative, we might argue that the narrator, in this string of aphorisms, interrupts a rather bizarre story first to address a Suisse Romande audience, then a universal audience in order to explain why the story is being told.

In all other instances it becomes difficult to ascertain the origin of the narrative in this novel's relatively few moments of sententiousness. For example, when the text affirms, "Regarder ce qui est, et ne rien mettre ici que ce qui est," it is conceivable that such a thought was constructed in the mind of the unnamed recorder of the events (34) and that it forms a natural part of narrated thought/speech. The same holds true for such utterances as "le goût de la destruction vous vient pour la seule destruction. Avant même qu'on soit ivre de vin, car il n'y a pas que cette ivresse ... Et il y a même un travail plus beau que de faire, une plus belle espèce de travail: c'est de défaire" (70). In this group of aphoristic formulations, either the characters (in this case the group of men destroying one of the town pubs) or the distant/anonymous narrative voice could be regarded as the authors of the thought. (See also 30, 31, 39, 50, 71, 75, 89, 90, 94, 96, 103, 107.)

A particularly intriguing case results from a reflection fashioned either in the consciousness of the users of a tramway (an element of the pure "narration") or by a wry narrator-author. In the final analysis, however, it probably matters little whose "voice" it is: "*Défense de parler au conducteur*: quand on ne lui parle pas c'est lui qui vous parle" (38). Perhaps this swift, incisive touch in Ramuz's word-painting might be construed as a sarcastic critique of commonplace utilitarian written texts designed more to "lay down the law" than to be art.

INSIGHTS GAINED FROM A SEPARATE LISTING OF THE NOVEL'S APHORISMS

All the major studies of Ramuz's work comment on the author's use, in his fictional texts, of primitive linguistic forms. Ramuz was often accused by the French literary establishment of simply not knowing how to write standard French. However, a few informed critics, among them his publisher Bernard Grasset, were able to contrast Ramuz's purely artistic creations with the polished Académie French of his non-fictional writings. They were able to deduce that Ramuz used unconventional syntax, lexicon, and morphology advisedly, in the interest of employing the primary resources of the French language for an innovative literary enterprise.

This same division, which might be summed up in terms of a contrast between Ramuz himself and the elements of the fictional narrative he has created, is borne out lingually by contrasting the various aphoristic passages in *Présence de la mort*. The string of aphorisms viewed previously, which might be entitled "heightened sensibility to the phenomena in the universe," are cast in learned French (16, 18, 24, 48). Most of the remaining ones, by contrast, are constructed with the banal "il y a" (30, 31, 31, 47, 70) and elements of spontaneous – that is, untreated – discourse ("ça," repetitions, "repairs," run-on sentences, etc.).

It is useful to consider several examples from among the aphorisms of *Présence de la mort* of the "unpolished," ostensibly primitive style that earned Ramuz either loyal supporters or staunch detractors:

C'est ce qui est beau; – étant plusieurs, n'étant qu'une seule personne.   (71, emphasis added)

Et salut! vite encore, parce que tu t'en vas, parce que tout s'en va, parce que rien doit durer, parce que rien ne peut durer, salut une dernière fois.   (90)

Jusqu'au bout, jusqu'au tout dernier moment, tant que tu pourras; tant qu'un petit reste de souffle te sera accordé, un rien de souffle encore, parce que le mot est court.   (94)

In neither of these two general categories, however, do we observe studied or contrived rhetorical strategies. The aphoristic utterances rely mainly on semantic content for their effect. While some of the aphorisms use subtle antitheses, they fail to strike the reader by any particular rhetorical brilliance:

car il y a ceux qui ont et ceux qui n'ont pas.   (47)

Le soleil prend à une place; à une autre, il donne.   (50)

des espèces de glaneurs en tout, n'étant des moissonneurs en rien.   (140)

Finally, a reading of all the aphoristic sentences or sentence fragments in this novel, which are usually cast in the universal present

tense, conveys a coherent flow of ideas. Were these aphoristic fragments not present in the text, we would be left with a report of
apocalyptic events, surreal characters, meagre dialogue, and some
perhaps memorable descriptions. Ramuz in his later works presents
precisely these elements, purged, however, of essay-like commentary.
What remains is an idiosyncratic juxtaposition of colours and expres-
sionist forms, reminiscent of Cézanne's later work. *Présence de la mort*
is particularly valuable to the reader who wants to discern, through
the greatest possible economy of means, the philosophical and artistic
underpinnings of Ramuz's literary production.

THE WORLD OF THE TEXT

The philosophical concerns dealt with in this novel, and which concerned Ramuz generally, are summed up neatly in the separate listing
of its aphorisms. In many cases the concern is obvious and requires
no particular analysis. Others have not been dealt with in the critical
literature. For example, all Ramuz's novels treat in some way the
complexities and "contradictions" of love (30, 31). All portray characters who, for sometimes inexplicable reasons, "have," while others
"have not." There is present in the Ramuzian text a longing – usually
unfulfilled – for human solidarity (71) and for the impossible return
to lost "innocence" (75). Extensive explorations of decay and death
inform the whole of the Ramuzian corpus; many of the aphorisms in
Présence de la mort express the author's preoccupations as concisely
as anywhere in his writings (70, 89, 90, 94, 96, 107).

Other of Ramuz's concerns are less evident, even less conventional,
and demand particular focus on the part of the reader. Before the
notoriety of the French existentialists Ramuz had already conceived
an idiosyncratic version of humanity and its "absurd" condition.
Ramuz has reduced the following reflections, taken from *Présence de
la mort*, to the strict essentials. With a deceptive simplicity they tell
in a few easy words what Sartre and Camus have described over
many pages employing heavy academic discourse:

comme on est seul pour mourir! Chaque chose, chaque être, seuls devant
rien.   (96)

On fait tout ce qu'on peut, on cherche à se défendre, même si ça ne doit
servir à rien.   (103)

Throughout his writings Ramuz proposes a unique *modus vivendi*
as one faces the prospect of ultimate nothingness. This aphoristic

exploration demonstrates tidily: "Les choses qu'on devra quitter, peut-être les aimer davantage. Et connaître enfin l'espace, le généreux, le varié, le large et long, l'abondant, le très vaste, – dans sa solitude et sa nudité" (24). These thoughts, at first glance perhaps no more than rudimentary jottings, found sophisticated vehicles of elaboration in Sartre's *L'Etre et le Néant* and Camus's *Le Mythe de Sisyphe*. One could argue, however, that Ramuz developed the same fundamental ideas no less fully, not by way of methodical philosophical investigation but through the agency of "blotches of colour" and with provocatively "awkward" lingual portraits and literary still-life drawings. Also, his conception of absurdity (see "Les aimer davantage") seems a more optimistic one than even Camus's.

Like Proust, Ramuz saw in art the possibility of capturing and prolonging the ephemeral (89). His model of the universe and of existence differs, however, in that it posits a continual "giving" and "taking" (50), an incessant, all-encompassing, creative tension between creation and destruction (90). As such, humanity must be satisfied with its lot as "des espèces de glaneurs en tout, n'étant des moissonneurs en rien" (140).

One final concern, related to the one above and on which Ramuz lays an unusually strong emphasis throughout his corpus, becomes evident in the "Denkökonomie" of *Présence de la mort*: "Nous sommes tellement balancés. Tellement portés, tout le temps, de l'une des extrémités de nous à l'autre extrémité. Qui sommes-nous? qui sommes-nous?" (120) This model of human personality – that is, of a being composed of extremes and driven to and fro by them – is succinctly enacted by Vittoz in *Présence de la mort*; during the final crisis he at once dresses as a woman, engages in fits of laughter, and rues the lost interest on his savings (112–17). In a more sustained manner Ramuz had already treated the theme of draconian alternation between opposing inner forces in *Jean-Luc persécuté* (1909).

CONCLUSION

After the portraiture of Vittoz, a chapter follows in which a captain of an erring ship and an aimless "promeneur" are briefly depicted. In Ramuz's later novels he would have left us only the word-painting of the image and refrained from any commentary on them. In *Présence de la mort*, however, we are still offered some aphoristic guideposts – albeit sparse ones – that aid in making sense of the expressionistically presented events and characters. Without these guideposts it would remain entirely up to the reader to establish his or her own chain of signification; or we might choose simply to contemplate the Cézanne-like artistry of the descriptions. However, in *Présence de la mort* Ramuz still consents to guide his reader from time to time. With regard to the Vittoz-captain-"promeneur" sequence, he inserts a key bit of evaluation. As a result of this addition, we are guided towards a more definite interpretation of the images than if the aphoristic commentary were not present. In consort with those images the reader, with the author, is also brought to reflect on the proposition that we are "carried, all the time, from one of our extremes to the other."

He does not stop there, however, and causes his reader, as a consequence of both the narration and the aphoristic reflection, to ask the quintessential question of all literature: "Qui sommes-nous?" (120)

Such a subtle approach to the Labovian narration-evaluation complex characterizes the whole of this novel. Although Ramuz has chosen the medium of the written word to realize his artistic vision, his writing progressively breaks out of the realm of literature and increasingly resembles the work of the visual artist. At no time during his career, though, except perhaps in his essays, can we consider Ramuz to be either a didactic writer or a writer *à thèse*. He neither creates brilliant and quotable "antagonistic" formulations nor advances propositions with a "moralistic" tinge. His late works put forward no propositions at all – not directly, at any rate. When such propositions do emerge in the earlier work, they tend to do so only out of the overriding attempt to paint "what is."

Indeed, Ramuz's credo as an artist-creator is summed up perhaps nowhere better than in that crucial aphoristic remark found in *Présence de la mort*: "Regarder ce qui est, et ne rien mettre ici que ce qui est" (34). We should not, however, be deceived by the apparent facility of this task, for Ramuz accomplishes his ends with a studied and highly disciplined balance of subjects, colors, shadings, perspectives, and proportions. This achievement proves the more remarkable in that it has been effected through "blotches" not of paint but of words.

Eventually, no "wordy" commentary is required at all. *Présence de la mort*, with its residue of aphoristic commentary, is none the less valuable as an antecedent to the later, purer approach, for it offers a relatively clear introduction to a particularly elusive world and an unusual "equipment for living."

9 *Neige noire*

The critical bibliography at the end of a selection of Hubert Aquin's essays, published in 1982 under the title *Blocs erratiques*, lists well over a hundred studies of various lengths on the author's work. A perusal of the topics covered indicates something of a critical morass.

In reviewing a 1987 collection of articles on Aquin, Cedric May quickly detects the difficulties associated with scholarly treatment of Aquin's texts: "Inevitably, I suspect, Aquin gets the last laugh from the grave. The contributors, though perfectly aware of the labyrinth of Aquin's writing, have been lured into it." May then contends: "But what we need when confronted with writing as complex as that of Aquin, ... compounded by [his] taste for occultation and literary conundrums, is an honest and unpretentious effort to elucidate" (388).

For these reasons it seems advisable, in the particular case of Aquin and his last novel, to concentrate on a single idea and examine it from various angles rather than become entangled in too many questions at once. Treating this single idea towards the end of our study will also provide a convenient avenue for rounding off the discussion of aphorism in the contemporary francophone novel.

A debate ensues when we consider, first, one of Rosmarin Heidenreich's conclusions repeated in two chapters on Aquin in *The Postwar Novel in Canada* (1989) and then compare Heidenreich's views with related statements by Aquin himself. She posits the "high indeterminacy" of Aquin's fiction and other postmodern Canadian authors' "obsession with the reader" (118). To summarize this line of argument, Heidenreich quotes a lengthy passage from Aquin's crucial essay "La Disparition élocutoire du poète" (1974).

However, engaged in a demonstration of the concept of "high indeterminacy" and reader-oriented texts, we might tend to neglect the "other half" present in all of Aquin's novels, particularly in *Neige noire*. In the very passage that Heidenreich quotes, Aquin hints at a complicating factor in literary creation: "Quand j'écris, je pense au lecteur comme *à la moitié de mon être*, et j'éprouve le besoin de le trouver et de l'investir" (118). Patricia Smart in her seminal *Hubert Aquin agent double* (1973) has taught us to expect in Aquin's text to encounter the mirror-image – the antithesis – of each of his ostensibly concrete, but in reality precarious, "affirmations."

Aquin himself sets out to demonstrate how complex the entire issue of writing, reading, and textual sense-making is. It seems that he would have us think deeper than "mere" indeterminacy. Let us consider a number of his dialectical views on the matter – not that these should "lay down the law" with regard to his own or any works of fiction, but simply this: in addition to elucidating his own works, Aquin's inquiry serves to enlarge our understanding of "literary phenomena" generally.

The first statement throws out a subtle challenge to the often dogmatic case contemporary critics make for textual indecipherability or indeterminacy. Aquin contends: "L'écriture, si insensée soit-elle à certains égards, a toujours un sens. Elle est dirigée vers un lecteur-juge qui confère de la valeur à ce qu'il reçoit et condamne au néant ce qu'il rejette" ("Disparition," 263). At the same time he asserts: "Je trouve que l'ego de l'écrivain doit évacuer au maximum l'écriture" (264).

At another place in the same essay Aquin argues in favour of a certain synthesis seldom achieved either in literary production or in criticism:

La littérature comporte deux versants: un versant intentionnel qui est celui de l'écriture et un versant manifeste correspondant à la lecture. Il arrive parfois, dans l'étude de la littérature, qu'on isole ni plus ni moins le versant intentionnel de l'auteur (comme dans une certaine psychocritique, par exemple); cela a pour conséquence de rendre inintelligible une intentionnalité dont on néglige le sens et le terme.

   Le rapport écriture-lecture est constitutif du phénomène littéraire. L'écriture est le négatif qui, passé au révélateur de la lecture, imprime une image dans la conscience. Sans révélateur, le négatif est condamné à rester opaque; et sans négatif à imprégner, le révélateur ne révèle rien.   (264)

Aquin's borrowings from the techniques of photography typify this thesis-antithesis-synthesis mode of thinking and writing. Throughout the essay he elaborates his thought in this Hegelian vein, so that when we arrive at his "concluding" *plaidoyer*, the subtle irony in his final reflection causes us to call into doubt any former straightforwardness: "Dans les livres contemporains québécois et autres, j'ai trouvé que l'auteur est décidément surprésent. Le livre se trouve, en fin de compte, contaminé par la présence de son auteur à tel point que le jeu, quand on lit, consiste à aimer ou à détester la personne même de l'auteur. J'en viens à préconiser une pratique de l'absence de telle sorte que les livres ne deviennent pas indiscernables à force d'être englués. A la limite, je me demande si la grande innovation littéraire ne serait pas de revenir à l'anonymat ... A lecteurs anonymes, auteurs anonymes" (297). The phraseology "A la limite" might be seen to indicate a certain sarcastic irony in Aquin's suggestion that we return to the former idea of entirely "anonymous" authors.

Finally, arriving at the core of the matter, Aquin asks two essential questions pertaining to the act of writing and to the reader's reception of it:

– Qu'est-ce qu'un lecteur recherche en abordant un roman ou une suite de romans?
– Le cinéma et la T.V. ne fournissent-ils pas les mêmes plaisirs, les mêmes émotions moyennant un effort moindre de sa part?   (265)

To conclude this initial portion of the discussion, we note that in spite of the "high indeterminacy" of Aquin's text we are presented both in his essays and in his narrative prose with a few signposts that, while offering no clear way out of the labyrinth, at least point the reader in certain directions. For example, we may think of the novel *Prochain épisode* as anything but aphoristic, and yet the text contains a significant number of pithy reflective-evaluative statements. This one is characteristic: "Tuer confère un style à l'existence" (23). Further, Aquin in his essays often causes a thematic strand to condense at some point into a concluding aphorism. For example, in the epistolary "Le Texte ou le silence marginal" Aquin makes an impassioned and tortuously argued case for writing as the vehicle *par excellence* for the achievement of selfhood and self-expression. Before proceeding to the next point, he stops to tie the disparate threads together with an aphorism: "On ne dénoncera jamais assez le prix exorbitant de l'individuation" (269).

In preparation for what is to follow, it is time to ask whether the visual arts, especially the medium of film, are capable of conveying such personalized, compactly expressed reflections, and of allowing the viewer/hearer the time to assimilate and respond to them.

THE NARRATOLOGICAL CONSEQUENCE OF APHORISM

Neige noire was published the same year as the essay "La Disparition élocutoire du poète." The novel's enigmatic epigraph and its unusual form may be better understood in light of this essay.

The epigraph to the text – an aphorism of Sören Kierkegaard – reads: "Je dois maintenant être et ne pas être." That the epigraph alludes to *Hamlet*, from which Aquin quotes extensively in the novel, is obvious. We are immediately reminded of the main character, Nicolas, and his inherent inability "to be." Contiguous to the character is the tenuous birth of the screenplay and, by extension, of the novel's own incapacity "to be." All these failures combine with Aquin's native Québec and its failure to exist. Finally, one is reminded of Aquin himself, at once present and absent in his final work, and of the fact that he ended his own life in 1977, not long after the book's publication. All the foregoing elements combine in such a way to produce not necessarily decipherability, but at the very least a remarkable coherence.

The novel itself is composed of two opposing faces. The first is a screenplay stripped of reflective elements – that is, a cinematographic camera presenting purposefully arranged sound-and-sight images in rapid succession. Aquin then interpolates at random completely separate segments of essayistic commentary. At times these segments seem to have nothing at all to do with the immediately contiguous screenplay (or, rather, narration in the form of a screenplay). Usually, however, these sections treat some nearby aspect of the text. Aquin sets the commentary off distinctly from the screenplay through the use of parentheses.

Claude Simon's *La Route des Flandres*, we recall, represents the opposite approach, in which reflective elements in the text are made as indistinguishable as possible from the rest of the narrative.

As regards a decision on what is aphorism and what is not amid the essay sections of *Neige noire*, we encounter the same problems as in Saint-Exupéry's *Terre des hommes*. All the statements in these lengthy sections use verbs in the present tense, and nearly every sentence could be construed as aphoristic. For the separate appendix it seemed sensible to choose only those statements that are particularly concentrated and provocative and that meet one or more of Fricke's criteria. In some cases, however, the selection is arbitrary and personal.

The formal structure Aquin chose for *Neige noire* (reflected also in the antithetical title) drastically partitions pure "narration" from pure "evaluation" and sharply enacts the "author present or not" dialectics. In one of the text's halves the author appears to be stepping aside; in the other we suddenly read nothing but "the author." René Lapierre, the compiler of *Blocs erratiques*, enunciates the conflict we are dealing with neatly in the form of a question: "S'agit-il enfin de l'affirmation ou la disparition de l'écrivain?" (257)

INSIGHTS GAINED FROM A SEPARATE LISTING OF THE NOVEL'S APHORISMS

As has often been the case in the other novels under study, Aquin tends to provoke a response from his reader through the combination of pithy formulation and superlatives. These should by now be easy to identify as we read through each of the aphoristic fragments from *Neige noire*.

Further, Aquin counts as still another twentieth-century writer who in some way came under the influence of Nietzsche. We know this to be so in his case because of an unpublished (and never aired) program Aquin prepared, entitled "Nietzsche," for Radio Canada (*Blocs erratiques*, Bibliographie critique). More than any other of the authors we have studied, Aquin seems to come closest to the "antagonistic," rhetorically dazzling style of Nietzsche. Witness the running subtle wordplays, many of which defy classification into any distinct rubric of tropes or rhetorical figures. The following illustrations, in which the relevant features are highlighted, require no extraneous commentary:

Le temps déporte tout selon un diagramme toujours pareil, connu de tous et pourtant difficile parfois à réinventer par le seul jeu de la mémoire. On ne *feuillette* pas le temps, c'est lui qui *effeuille* nos vies.   (125)

Oui, le *temps transitif* coule selon une *transience frénatrice*, alors que l'autre, le *temps immanent* de la joie et de l'amour, se définit comme *l'haleine de la beauté*.   (127)

Je n'étais pas, j'ai été, je me souviens, je ne suis plus.   (138)

le Québec est en creux. Son éclipse récurrente fait penser à *l'absence d'une présence*, à un mystère inachevé.   (143)

la fiction n'est pas un *piège*, c'est elle, plutôt, qui est *piégée* par une réalité qu'elle ne contenait pas et qui l'envahit hypocritement.   (155)

L'amour donne le *vertige*, mais son *vertige*, si intolérable qu'il soit, est un *délice infini*. (264)

Aquin also reveals himself to be fond of the purportedly more Germanic *Schlusspointe*. The technique involves an innocuous reflection with some sort of mordant surprise at the end: "Les livres se ferment et s'ouvrent sans douleur, sans problème, tout au plus avec un petit craquement de l'épine. De plus, ils ne voient rien; ce sont des objets aveugles *comme leurs auteurs*" (235–6, emphasis added; see also 132, 167, 174, 194, 264).

As with Claude Simon and the reflective fragments of his text, Aquin shies away in his aphorisms from preachments and from facile signifier-signified relationships; rather, he composes dialectical philosophical investigations in the evasively provocative manner of Nietzsche.

THE WORLD OF THE TEXT

Although sustained attention will be devoted only to the topic of literary creation, reader response, and (in)determinacy, some of the more obvious elements of the "world" that *Neige noire* attempts to project should be pointed out in passing.

First, it is useful to be aware of an interesting convergence. In "La Disparition élocutoire du poète" Aquin speaks in terms analogous to those of Ricœur and Burke when he posits the "écriture-lecture" complex as a "condensé de la vie" – indeed, as a metaphor for life itself (266).

With Claude Simon, Aquin demonstrates in *Neige noire*, through his essayistic/aphoristic reflection on the separate screenplay, his preoccupation with the notion of time and movement. The content of the relevant aphorisms (28, 48, 69–70, 125, 127, 157, and 205) is easy to grasp. This group of reflections on spatio-temporal relationships forms a literary complement to the "raw," untreated cinematographic images that make up the screenplay.

More difficult to probe are Aquin's rather nihilistic reflections on love. These too are to be contemplated in conjunction with the novel's actual love scenes, which range from tender to brutally violent and involve the characters Nicolas, Sylvie, Eva, and Michel in various pairings. (See 79, 244, 264.) This rather grim part of Aquin's world might be adequately summed up in one concentrated sentence from the "reflective" portion of the text: "L'amour, si délibérément intrusif soit-il, se ramène à une approximation vélaire de l'autre, à une croisière désespérante sur le toit d'une mer qu'on ne peut jamais percer" (195).

A lone, highly unusual aphorism on the use of "the tabular present" deserves particular attention, given the underlying concern in this study with narratology and with the concepts of foregrounding and backgrounding: "(On emploie le présent pour faire l'inventaire de ce qui manque. Ce présent tabulaire évoque des lacunes, des creux, des omissions, des absences)" (241). This reflection has no clear referent in the text, whereas most of the other parenthetical bits of commentary pertain to immediately preceding events (e.g., 243). Because Aquin in this instance seems to leave the question of a referent open, it is tempting to construe *le présent* as the present tense – as opposed to other tenses – in a text. If we follow through on such an approach, Aquin's reasons for "employing the present" prove fascinating. One might reword the sentence to say something like "One breaks away from the other narrative tenses and uses the present in order to 'evoke' [but not necessarily fill in] gaps, blanks, omissions, and absences" in the narrative.

The question of Quebec's precarious, fragmented process of individuation and the way this thematic strand is interwoven with that of the screenplay emerges overtly only once. It is significant that the unusual overtness emanates from an aphoristic reflection: "le Québec est en creux. Son éclipse récurrente fait penser à l'absence d'une présence, à un mystère inachevé" (143).

In this aphorism Aquin again plays with intertext and language when he inverts the title of Rina Lasnier's well-known collection of poems *Présence de l'absence* (1956). Understanding this subtle "intention" – or ploy – within the reflective half of the text causes a significant part of its pure narration (the screenplay) to fall into place. For example, we may at first be baffled by the constant switches in the novel from the "space" of Montréal to that of Norway, and ask why Aquin would have chosen Norway as a figure of existential escape and exile.

After detecting how Aquin uses intertextual references in an aphorism, we come to understand how the process works in other passages throughout the novel. Seeing himself and perhaps the whole of his nation as a projection of the "poète maudit" – of whom Emile Nelligan is commonly regarded in Québec letters as the archetype – Aquin quotes in *Neige noire* from his predecessor's famous poem "Soir d'hiver." The fragment is inserted into the novel with no preparation and no follow-up and is set off visually by large spaces, by the ubiquitous "reflective" parentheses, and by quotation marks: "('Je suis la nouvelle Norvège')" (192).

It is then enlightening to view the context from which Aquin lifted the fragment: "Tous les étangs gisent gelés, mon âme est noire: Où vis-je? où vais-je? Tous ses espoirs gisent gelés: *Je suis la nouvelle*

Norvège d'où les blonds ciels s'en sont allés" (42, emphasis added). The foregoing analysis might serve in part to elucidate Aquin's unusually caustic, enigmatic closing statement, which is aphoristic in nature: "Enfuyons-nous vers notre seule patrie! Que la vie plénifiante qui a tissé ces fibrilles, ces rubans arciformes, ces ailes blanches de l'âme, continue éternellement vers le point oméga que l'on n'atteint qu'en mourant et en perdant toute identité, pour renaître et vivre dans le Christ de la Révélation" (264).

One's hope, one's planned destination is far away, so far removed from onerous reality that it finally dissipates – is sublimated – into a kind of exotic mysticism. All these issues, however, cohere with the topic of textual sense-making. Might Aquin be suggesting that contemporary readers wallow in indeterminacy, when an "honest and unpretentious effort to elucidate" might better serve in order "to be"?

We are then left with the bulk of the aphorisms, which explore in some way the *raison d'être* of literature and the locutionary – the speaker-addressee – dialectics (28, 51, 91, 154, 155, 157, 167, 174, 199, 230, 235–6). Each of these statements calls for extended commentary and analysis, especially in the light of current debates on literary and critical theory. However, because of the "overview" nature of this study I must limit analysis only to Aquin's fundamental ideas in the domain. The reader is therefore referred to all the aphoristic fragments cited above. As a coherent "chain" they conduct a lively and trenchant discussion on the topic.

It seems appropriate to begin the trajectory with one of the novel's earliest pieces of reflective aphoristic commentary: "Cette spécificité cinématographique est d'ailleurs infiniment séduisante: elle ressemble à l'aventure aléatoire de chaque individu. La vie ne permet pas d'aller bien loin, non plus que d'approfondir le sens de tout ce qui est. L'être humain, si doué soit-il, reste toujours à l'extérieur de ce qu'il veut percer" (28).

Aquin first presents enough alternation of screenplay and parenthetical commentary to allow the reader to become familiar with the technique. Once this task is accomplished, the above aphorism posits overtly and in concise form the key dualism of the novel: on the one hand the cinematographic, "aleatoric" nature of individual experience, and on the other the individual's drive to reflect upon, "cut through," and "fathom" the resulting perceptions. However, in the "world" that *Neige noire* is attempting to project the two operations remain strictly partitioned one from another. The very layout of the text thus serves to enact what Aquin considers a fundamental irreconcilability. The reader, of course, is free to go beyond the logic of the text and to ask whether the two phenomena really are condemned to remain so drastically estranged from each other.

One final detail from the immediately foregoing passage requires further attention. Aquin's use of the adjective *séduisante* to describe the powers of the cinema to represent human experience and perception presages his opposing views, which come later in the text, on this very topic (see also 51). Indeed, as the novel unfolds, Aquin casts progressively more doubt on the supposed miracle of cinematography. The following piece of commentary, found towards the middle of the work, quite explicitly reveals the mirror-image, or the opposite side of the text's initial enthusiasm for the medium: "Le film, mieux que tout autre moyen d'expression, rend bien cette fluidité achérontique, dans la mesure au moins où il ne s'arrête jamais avant la fin de sa propre projection ... Donc, vingt-quatre images par seconde réussissent pour que le spectateur n'aperçoive ni les rivets, ni les collures, ni les pales de l'obturateur. Cette poudre nyctalope s'introduit dans le cerveau du spectateur et lui permet de reconstituer le fleuve temporaire qui nous conduit tous à la mort" (157; see also 167, 174, 176). Nyctalopia is a visual disorder in which one can *only* see at night. Astonishingly, Aquin equates the uninterrupted bombardment of unreflected phenomena with a disorder and, ultimately, with death.

Significantly, Aquin waits until the end of the novel – but even then only tentatively – to rehabilitate "the word" and written "fiction:"

La parole engendre, elle ne fait pas qu'orner ou accompagner l'existence. (199)

La fiction, plus large que la vérité parce qu'indéterminée, englobe accidentellement la vérité.   (230)

Finally, the text's commentary on the topic of literary creation and on the author-text polarity converges in this aphorism: "Les livres se ferment et s'ouvrent sans douleur, sans problème, tout au plus avec un petit craquement de l'épine. De plus, ils ne voient rien; ce sont des objets aveugles comme leurs auteurs" (235–6).

Aquin's equation here of book and author is far from innocent. The underlying allusive portion of the remark at once posits authors' fragility – their vulnerability – and then almost masochistically rues the fact. Through the open confession that they are "blind" (an evocation of Oedipus?) Aquin would want us to believe, at the very least, in the tragic lucidity of authors and the books they create. If taken further, Aquin is making a caustic plea for authors, books, and a thoughtful readership.

CONCLUSION

If Aquin does indeed assert his presence from time to time in his
works of imaginative prose, his preferred medium for doing so is
essayistic, or aphoristic, discourse. It is at these moments within his
novels that he involves the reader most intensely and, through
sophisticated rhetorical means, goads us into some kind of response.
The aphorisms, too, teach us to avoid hasty judgments or conclusions
about any given "track" within Aquin's work – or any literary work,
for that matter. This appeal for caution applies particularly to Aquin's
text: for each "action" we usually find some kind of opposite "reac-
tion." However, between these poles, complex syntheses are constantly being effected. All these "tracks" in turn intersect with one
another to form a dynamic, highly coherent whole.

10 Conclusion

Aphorism, while constituting a literary genre *per se*, can function concomitantly with a different genre – for example, the novel. Aphorisms deployed along with another genre serve both as a component of the overall text and as text in and of themselves. Given their differentiated identity, aphorisms display idiosyncratic powers of evocation peculiar to the genre. Because of its peculiar behaviour in relation to the narrated chain of events, aphorism often demands the reader's focused attention. Once a reader becomes conscious of their rhetorical and semantic content, a novel's aphorisms might do little more than support a traditional reading of the text. In other cases, however, concerted focus on a given novel's chain of aphorisms might help to provide evidence for a specifically located reading, or perhaps engender entirely new readings of the text.

When concentrating on a novel's aphorisms, we must consider how this subgenre, acting in partnership with the novel, might contribute to the coherence of the overall discourse. For the sake of orderly investigation, throughout this study I have largely defined the notions of narration, evaluation, backgrounding – and even the aphorisms themselves – as disparate entities within a novel. In novelistic discourse, however, aphorisms form only one of many elements in a network of coherence. This is to say that none of the diverse elements in a novel can be removed, then viewed in total isolation, without disturbing the text's global drive and sense of unity.

Since no detailed scholarly investigation has previously been undertaken on aphorism in the contemporary novel written in

French, the principal aim of this study is to demonstrate first that the genre is alive and well, as much so as when the *moralistes* were writing. This finding is not as self-evident as is generally supposed. Second, in a thoroughgoing manner we have seen how aphorism performs a key sense-making function within narrative prose. In some texts aphorisms may contribute heavily to a novel's coherence, while in others reported events, characterizations, dialogue, description, or essayistic commentary will assume more prominent cohering roles.

August Wilhelm Beutel summarizes all the above with considerable wit. In a spoof on the genre of aphorism he revises a definition found in Johannes Hoffmeister's *Wörterbuch der philosophischen Begriffe*. The original posits as qualifying criteria for the genre: "in sich abgeschlossen" and "nicht mit anderen Sätzen verbunden" ("self-contained" and "unrelated to other sentences"). Beutel counters, however, with "Ohne 'die anderen Sätze' gäbe es zwar den Aphorismus: Wörter: aber inhaltlos." (Without "the other sentences" there might well be an aphorism: words: but without content. 5, translation mine.)

Next, we need to consider the relationship that might exist between aphorisms in a given novel and aphorisms in other contexts. This notion becomes particularly crucial when we elect to view a novel as a product of a "national" literature or to situate it within a body of texts written in a given language. A.L. Becker's challenging assertion helps to shed light on aphorism as a literary-historical phenomenon in the specific case of modern francophone novels. He says: "Part of the context of any text is, more or less, all previous texts in a particular culture, especially texts considered to be in the same genre; readable literature is structurally coherent with its own ancestors" (212).

For the sake of argument let us subscribe to Becker's rather strong version of intertext and look at some of the "ancestors" in question. In the case of francophone civilization, literary texts could hardly avoid being aware of – if not constrained by – perhaps the most illustrious tradition of sententious writing in Western civilization, namely the loosely defined group we refer to as the *moralistes*.

In a later period Stendhal broke much new ground in French letters when he injected not the usual "integrative" maxim/aphorism into his novels but rather the "antagonistic" version of the genre. It might be iteresting to note in passing that the sustained use of the antagonistic aphorism within *Le Rouge et le Noir* demonstrably influenced the thought and style of Nietzsche. Flaubert went still a step further as he systematically incorporated aphoristic *lieux communs* into

Madame Bovary with the intent of exposing their vacuous content. Other authors and movements could be mentioned, but these three of themselves continue to bear inestimably upon francophone writers in the twentieth century, either directly or indirectly.

It should therefore not be surprising to encounter aphoristic formulation of both types, integrative and antagonistic, in much contemporary French-language fiction. When a contemporary aphorism undertakes to revise a previous one or to challenge an entrenched proverb, a clear and direct line of intertext is revealed, and Becker's seemingly overstated line of argument is at least in part substantiated.

To tie up a number of loose ends, it is useful in these concluding statements to consider aphorism as a tripartite phenomenon – as (1) the *creation* of an author who has chosen a certain (2) *medium* (in this case the novel) and has addressed himself or herself to an (3) anonymous *audience*. Perhaps more efficiently than any other scholar, Fricke identifies many of the techniques whereby aphorism serves, in genre-specific ways, to provoke a reader/hearer into taking note of, then coming to terms with the text.

Since the advent of the New Critics we have been taught the futility of ascribing actual intention to an author in relation to his or her text. That a text-builder has consciously contrived and purposefully deployed a given aphorism may form a tempting proposition, but in most cases such intent is unverifiable. It is wiser to think of aphorism simply as one of many possible "mediums" that can bear more or less heavily upon a narrative, regardless of authorial intent.

For example, aphorisms can comment on the narration, perhaps even allude to the point of the story. However, literary texts by their very nature preclude any negotiation of meaning between creator and text-recipient; in written discourse the task of sense-making has been shifted on to an anonymous reader. In the twentieth century novelists seem to have drifted farther and farther away from a conception of aphorism as "laying down the law," or of providing a built-in, author/ized interpretation to their texts. It seems more productive, therefore, to suggest that because of their pithy, often provocative constitution, aphorisms often act as a particularly incisive initiator of a reader-oriented hermeneutical process.

On to another general question we attempted to answer: Do any general tendencies emerge as we view contemporary authors' use of aphorism in the francophone novel? Fricke's, and to a certain extent John Gross's attempts at a *Gattungsbestimmung* (at defining the genre) prove useful in identifying the various mechanisms at work in an aphorism. Proceeding from this definition process are a variety of indicators of potential help in the sense-making process. However, the diversity of approaches in the modern francopohone novel speaks against methodically submitting each text to a Procrustean bed designed by, say, Fricke. Instead, it is more beneficial to see his and others' contributions to the field of research on aphorism for what they are: not as rigid taxonomies but as an extensive presentation of inherent tendencies.

In this respect few common or general patterns emerge from the overview taken by this study. At most it appears that many authors of French-language texts remain attracted to a favourite technique of the *moralistes* – namely, to formulate propositions that contain hyperbole or superlatives in one form or another. This loose group of writers, however, with the exception of the atypically straightforward Saint-Exupéry, often lace their "sententious" propositions with some form of irony. They thereby deconstruct any maxim-like exaggeration before it is able to carry out any "integrative" function. This move demonstrates clearly a hallmark of the Gallic character, expressed concisely in the colloquial proverb "Il ne faut pas exagérer."

Such aphoristic formulations become perhaps more constative remarks than rules of behaviour. "Texts" thus conceived help to project a "world" or to bring to light recurring situations, but in most cases do not prescribe solutions or "lay down the law."

Lastly, when considering aphorisms in a given novel, we must confront the issue of referentiality. In more expansive terms: what is the relationship between aphorism as a literary event and events in the real world? Since Stendhal, Flaubert, Nietzsche, and Joyce, many francophone novelists have led the way in shattering the notion that a literary text should or can refer to a clear, extratextual signified. As an alternative, contemporary novelists have frequently endeavoured to create self-referential texts.

Accordingly, particularly in the francophone "new novel," we observe aphorisms that explore the act of writing, literary phenomena, textual representation of "reality," and the deferral of meaning with each new reading. However, even postmodern narratives (at least those in French) seem hardly able to resist the temptation here and there to insert pithy interventions conceived in the mould of their *moraliste* predecessors. Generally speaking, though, in the case of the contemporary novel written in French, the text-builder affords the reader more freedom than before to imagine a personalized "world," rather than referring him or her to a rigidly conceived set of circumstances outside the text.

To conclude, we may do well observe a few aphoristic formulations taken from an entirely different set of well-known novels. The selection is personal and arbitrary. Any novel could have been chosen.

Bear in mind the immediately foregoing discussion on textual constraints; reflect on how each fragment might function within the
overall narrative; consider how the aphorism might bear the stamp
and style of the author who created it; speculate on the ways it can
provide relatively quick access to a "world," or to an "equipment for
living."

Anne Hébert's *Kamouraska* generally eschews aphoristic reflexivity.
A few striking examples, however, do appear in the last pages of the
work – for example, these two:

Qui ose répéter le mot "amour" et le mot "liberté" dans l'ombre, sans mourir
de désespoir?   (241)

Mourir une fois, deux fois, à l'infini jusqu'à ce que ce soit la dernière fois.
La vie n'est pas autre chose après tout.   (247)

Albert Camus concludes *La Peste*, a text often held to be eminently
pessimistic, with "on apprend au milieu des fléaux, qu'il y a dans les
hommes plus de choses à admirer que de choses à mépriser" (279).
Perhaps nowhere in all of French literature, least of all with the often
skeptical *moralistes*, is such an overtly promising view of humanity
presented.

The "new novelist" Nathalie Sarraute frequently ascribes aphoristic thoughts to the consciousness of her ostensibly vacuous characters
of *Le Planétarium*. These characters can frequently surprise us, as their
comments remind us of La Bruyère's *Les Caractères*. The straightforward, quasi-moralizing tone emanates from a narrative voice that is
difficult to identify: "on néglige stupidement les gens qu'on aime le
plus, on croit qu'il suffit de savoir qu'ils existent, on est sûr d'eux"
(142).

In Nicole Brossard's multifarious postmodern text *Le Désert mauve*
we are offered a few signposts that help to make sense of the text's
intricate complexities. The following sentence, which may be seen as
such a guidepost, inaugurates one of the chapters: "La peur est une
réalité qui encombre la fiction car sans elle nous jonglerions avec nos
vies bien au-delà de la leçon" (108/162).* In a sort of pre-reading
exercise Brossard from the outset allows the attentive reader to think
about and associate the concepts "peur/fiction/jongler/vie." This
move makes the subsequent reading of the chapter far less daunting.

One of the very few aphoristic comments in Robbe-Grillet's *La
Jalousie* characterizes both the way events are reported in the novel

---

* Brossard's novel uses two systems of pagination.

and the whole of his *nouveau roman* project. For the sake of clarity the corresponding bit of narration from the novel is included: "Franck balaye ainsi d'un seul coup les fictions qu'ils viennent d'échafauder ensemble. Rien ne sert de faire des suppositions contraires, puisque *les choses sont ce qu'elles sont: on ne change rien à la réalité*" (83, emphasis added).

Robbe Grillet's reflection, when taken with a small dose (probably unintended) of irony, might also append a fitting *pointe* to a scholarly study of aphorism as it functions in contemporary works of francophone fiction. Perhaps the only reality that can be demonstrated is that aphorism is present in the French-language novel of the twentieth century. However, this study lays no definitive claim to *truth* about how and why they were created or about their relationship to the surrounding elements of discourse. Rather, it proposes several of many possible avenues of exploration and elucidation. In a field where little research and analysis have been carried out, it is wise to subscribe to the "conclusion" of Geoffrey Bennington's book and, as he did, "look proleptically toward further work, to local testings and modifications of the gestures elaborated here" (209).

Appendices

A *Terre des hommes*

La terre nous en apprend plus long sur nous que tous les livres. (9)

L'homme se découvre quand il se mesure avec l'obstacle. (9)

Il faut bien tenter de se rejoindre. (10)

[La terre:] la seule planète véritable, ... la nôtre, ... celle qui, seule, cont[ient] nos paysages familiers, nos maisons amies, nos tendresses. (28)

Les nécessités qu'impose un métier, transforment et enrichissent le monde. (33)

Ainsi va la vie. Nous nous sommes enrichis d'abord, nous avons planté pendant des années, mais viennent les années où le temps défait ce travail et déboise. Les camarades, un à un, nous retirent leur ombre. Et à nos deuils se mêle désormais le regret secret de vieillir. (40)

La grandeur d'un métier est, peut-être, avant tout, d'unir des hommes: il n'est qu'un luxe véritable, et c'est celui des relations humaines. (40)

En travaillant pour les seuls biens matériels, nous bâtissons nous-mêmes notre prison. Nous nous enfermons solitaires, avec notre monnaie de cendre qui ne procure rien qui vaille de vivre. (40)

Alors on s'épaule l'un l'autre. On découvre que l'on appartient à la même communauté. On s'élargit par la découverte d'autres consciences. On se regarde avec un grand sourire. on est semblable à ce prisonnier délivré qui s'émerveille de l'immensité de la mer. (43)

Quiconque lutte dans l'unique espoir de biens matériels, en effet, ne récolte rien qui vaille de vivre. (58)

Pour saisir le monde aujourd'hui nous usons d'un langage qui fut établi pour le monde d'hier. Et la vie du passé nous semble mieux répondre à notre nature, pour la seule raison qu'elle répond mieux à notre langage. (58)

Il semble que la perfection soit atteinte non quand il n'y a plus rien à ajouter, mais quand il n'y a plus rien à retrancher. (60)

La perfection de l'invention confine ainsi à l'absence d'invention. Et de même que, dans l'instrument, toute mécanique apparente s'est peu à peu effacée, et qu'il nous est livré un objet aussi naturel qu'un galet poli par la mer, il est également admirable que, dans son usage même, la machine peu à peu se fasse oublier. (60)

Au delà de l'outil, et à travers lui, c'est la vieille nature que nous retrouvons, celle du jardinier, du navigateur, ou du poète. (61)

Dans un monde où la vie rejoint si bien la vie, où les fleurs dans le lit même du vent se mêlent aux fleurs, où le cygne connaît tous les cygnes, les hommes seuls bâtissent leur solitude. (67)

Dans quel mince décor se joue ce vaste jeu des haines, des amitiés, des joies humaines! D'où les hommes tirent-ils ce goût d'éternité, hasardés comme ils sont sur une lave encore tiède, et déjà menacés par les sables futures, menacés par les neiges? Leurs civilisations ne sont que fragiles dorures: un volcan les efface, une mer nouvelle, un vent de sable. (67–8)

Nous habitons une planète errante. (69)

Ah! le merveilleux d'une maison n'est point qu'elle vous abrite ou vous réchauffe, ni qu'on en possède les murs. Mais bien qu'elle ait lentement déposé en nous ces provisions de douceur. Qu'elle forme, dans le fond du cœur, ce massif obscur dont naissent, comme des eaux de source, les songes. (77–8)

Il est si grave de passer à l'état de jeune fille à l'état de femme. (87)

Et les biens de la terre glissent entre les doigts comme le sable fin des dunes. (90)

L'écoulement du temps, d'ordinaire, n'est pas ressenti par les hommes. Ils vivent dans une paix provisoire. (90)

L'empire de l'homme est intérieur. (91)

Une femme invisible peut enchanter … toute une maison. Un puits porte loin, comme l'amour. (92)

Poussés par cette haine, ou cet amour. (112)

Des hommes qui ont vécu longtemps d'un grand amour, puis en furent privés, se lassent parfois de leur noblesse solitaire. Ils se rapprochent humblement de la vie, et, d'un amour médiocre, font leur bonheur. Ils ont trouvé doux d'abdiquer, de se faire serviles, et d'entrer dans la paix des choses. L'esclave fait son orgueil de la braise du maître.   (116)

Mais qu'il est difficile de faire demi-tour quand on marchait peut-être vers la vie!   (152)

Mais il faut oublier certaines images.   (160)

Et il ne s'agit pas de vivre dangereusement. Cette formule est prétentieuse. Les toréadors ne me plaisent guère. Ce n'est pas le danger que j'aime. Je sais ce que j'aime. C'est la vie.   (179)

Eau, tu n'as ni goût, ni couleur, ni arôme, on ne peut pas te définir, on te goûte, sans te connaître. Tu n'es pas nécessaire à la vie: tu es la vie. Tu nous pénètres d'un plaisir qui ne s'explique point par les sens. Avec toi rentrent en nous tous les pouvoirs auxquels nous avions renoncé. Par ta grâce, s'ouvrent en nous toutes les sources taries de notre cœur.

Tu es la plus grande richesse qui soit au monde, et tu es aussi la plus délicate, toi si pure au ventre de la terre. On peut mourir à deux pas d'un lac d'eau salée. On peut mourir malgré deux litres de rosée qui retiennent en suspens quelques sels. Tu n'acceptes point de mélange, tu ne supportes point d'altération, tu es une ombrageuse divinité.   (187)

Plus rien ne saurait prévaloir contre un sentiment de plénitude qui satisfait en nous je ne sais quel besoin essentiel que nous ne nous connaissions pas.   (189)

Tout est paradoxal chez l'homme, on le sait bien. On assure le pain de celui-là pour lui permettre de créer et il s'endort, le conquérant victorieux s'amollit, le généreux, si on l'enrichit, devient ladre.   (190)

Que nous importe les doctrines politiques qui prétendent épanouir les hommes, si nous ne connaissons d'abord quel type d'homme elles épanouiront. Qui va naître?   (190)

Nous ne sommes pas un cheptel à l'engrais, et l'apparition d'un Pascal pauvre pèse plus lourd que la naissance de quelques anonymes prospères.   (190)

L'essentiel, nous ne savons pas le prévoir. Chacun de nous a connu les joies les plus chaudes là où rien ne les promettait. Elles nous ont laissé une telle nostalgie, si nos misères les ont permises. Nous avons tous goûté, en retrouvant des camarades, l'enchantement des mauvais souvenirs.   (190)

La vérité, ce n'est point ce qui se démontre.   (190)

La logique? Qu'elle se débrouille pour rendre compte de la vie. (191)

J'ai trahi mon but si j'ai paru vous engager à admirer d'abord les hommes. Ce qui est admirable d'abord, c'est le terrain qui les a fondés. (191)

Certes les vocations aident l'homme à se délivrer: Mais il est également nécessaire de délivrer les vocations. (192)

La nostalgie, c'est le désir d'on ne sait quoi ... Il existe, l'objet du désir, mais il n'est point de mots pour le dire. (201)

Mais il existe une altitude des relations où la reconnaissance comme la pitié perdent leur sens. C'est là que l'on respire comme un prisonnier délivré. (201)

Ce sont les terres qui savent reconnaître le blé. (202)

Liés à nos frères par un but commun et qui se situe en dehors de nous, alors seulement nous respirons et l'expérience nous montre qu'aimer ce n'est point regarder l'un l'autre mais regarder ensemble dans la même direction. (203)

Tous, sous les mots contradictoires, nous exprimons les mêmes élans. Nous nous divisons sur des méthodes qui sont les fruits de nos raisonnements, non sur les buts: ils sont les mêmes. (203)

Pour comprendre l'homme et ses besoins, pour le connaître dans ce qu'il a d'essentiel, il ne faut pas opposer l'une à l'autre l'évidence de vos vérités. Oui, vous avez raison. Vous avez tous raison. (205)

On peut ranger les hommes en hommes de droite et en hommes de gauche, en bossus et en non bossus, en fascistes et en démocrates, et ces distinctions sont inattaquables. Mais la vérité, vous le savez, c'est ce qui simplifie le monde et non ce qui crée le chaos. La vérité, c'est ce qui dégage l'universel. (206)

La vérité, ce n'est point ce qui se démontre, c'est ce qui simplifie. (206)

Un mauvais élève du cours de Spéciales en sait plus long sur la nature et sur les lois que Descartes et Pascal. Est-il capable des mêmes démarches de l'esprit? (207)

Tous, plus ou moins confusément, éprouvent le besoin de naître. Mais il est des solutions qui trompent. Certes on peut animer les hommes, en les habillant d'uniformes. Alors ils chanteront leurs cantiques de guerre et rompront leur pain entre camarades. Ils auront retrouvé ce qu'ils cherchent, le goût de l'universel. Mais du pain qui leur est offert, ils vont mourir. (208)

La victoire est à qui pourrira le dernier. Et les deux adversaires pourrissent ensemble. (209)

Mais nous n'avons pas besoin de la guerre pour trouver la chaleur des épaules voisines dans une course vers le même but. (209)

Et s'il est bon que des civilisations s'opposent pour favoriser des synthèses nouvel tes, il est monstrueux qu'elles s'entredévorent. (209)

Quand nous prendrons conscience de notre rôle, même le plus effacé, alors seulement nous serons heureux.   (210)

Ce petit lot de traditions, de concepts et de mythes qui constitue toute la différence qui sépare Newton ou Shakespeare de la brute des cavernes.   (213)

Un animal vieilli conserve sa grâce. Pourquoi cette belle argile humaine est-elle abîmée?   (216)

Quand il naît par mutation dans les jardins une rose nouvelle, voilà tous les jardiniers qui s'émeuvent. On isole la rose, on cultive la rose, on la favorise. Mais il n'est point de jardinier pour les hommes. (217)

Il ne s'agit point de s'attendrir sur une plaie éternellement rouverte. (217)

Seul l'Esprit, s'il souffle sur la glaise, peut créer l'Homme.   (218)

B *Alexandre Chenevert*

Stars indicate the authorial-narrative voice.

Alliés, ennemis, alliés. (14)

Un homme ne devrait pas penser; ou bien ne pas avoir à éliminer les déchets. (15)

L'Anglais ... c'[est] l'ennemi héréditaire, proposé par l'histoire, l'école, l'entourage, celui dont [on] pourrait à peine se passer, tant, en le perdant, ses griefs manqueraient d'emploi. (19)

☆　Sans les morts, les absents, les peuplades jamais visitées, que deviendrait chez l'homme la faculté d'aimer! (21)

L'homme moderne hérit[e] d'une montagne de connaissances. Et où [est] la vérité, dans cette masse d'écrits? (23)

☆　Le nombre incroyable d'affections auxquelles un être humain est sujet. (26)

Esclavage pour esclavage, y [a]-t-il lieu d'en préférer une forme à l'autre? (27)

Un instant dévoré par le désir de changer le monde et de se changer soi-même, l'homme se découvr[e] une minute plus tard impuissant à seulement faire taire un chien. (30)

Tout [est] gratuit, sauf peut-être le malheur. (31)

☆　Cette quiétude morne que donne l'absence de tout espoir. (34)

☆　Un petit homme à sa place, quoi de plus invisible! (42)

[A]-t-on jamais entendu parler dans le monde d'un poète pauvre, crevant de faim, qui eût voulu changer de place avec un caissier? (45)

"L'amabilité!" (49)

[Est]-ce donc inévitablement par ce qu'on aim[e] le moins en soi que l'on rest[e] si bien lié aux autres?   (51)

Jamais dans le siècle il ne f[aut] cesser d'être sur ses gardes.   (61)

☆   Si les gens se vantent souvent d'être plus malheureux qu'ils ne sont, par contre, exagèrent-ils jamais les raisons de leur bien-être? (65)

L'expérience, vérité somme toute incommunicable.   (65)

On [a] découvert ces dernières années que la musique apaise les nerfs.   (71)

Les anges qui l'avaient louée au-dessus de l'étable de Bethlehem ne s'attendaient peut-être pas à la grande fatigue que serait pour les hommes du vingtième siècle l'exercice de la bonne volonté.   (72)

☆   Ce genre d'hommes qui résistent à une influence même s'ils la reconnaissent bonne dans leur fort intérieur, par besoin d'affirmer un esprit d'indépendance qu'ils ne possèdent pas.   (74)

☆   Mais quelle chance l'homme a-t-il de rencontrer parmi les millions d'habitants du globe son Ame sœur qui est peut-être un Chinois ou un Australien.   (75)

Partager un parapluie sous-entend la confiance et l'intimité de part et d'autre; peut-on imaginer deux hommes hérissés l'un contre l'autre jusqu'au fond de l'âme et allant sous le même parapluie!   (76)

Où va la vie, elle, précieuse unique? Il n'en [a] été donné qu'une à chaque homme. Pourquoi une seule? Si l'homme en avait une deuxième, de celle-ci arriverait-il à tirer quelque chose qui en valait la peine? Une seule vie, c'[est] à la fois trop court et trop long pour être utilisable ... Dieu n'avait pas été fort généreux.   (82)

Car on a beau dire d'un cerveau humain qu'il est un instrument merveilleux, il reste qu'on ne sait pas à quoi s'en tenir avec cet instrument.   (83–4)

Certains hommes d'affaires aiment donner l'impression qu'eux seuls, en raison des difficultés de l'ascension, [ont] ce qu'il faut pour parvenir.   (89–90)

☆   L'homme n'a pas encore commencé à percevoir les infinies possibilités de son destin sur terre.   (102)

☆   La tendre et mensongère voix humaine lorsqu'elle promet que tout ira mieux.   (106)

A se grouper ... étroitement, les médecins donnent l'impression d'être très forts contre la douleur.   (109)

Ne [vaut-il] pas mieux en ce monde être malade plutôt que malheureux[?]   (110)

☆   Ces ennuis de santé communs à un certain âge de la femme, pour ainsi dire naturels, sans grand intérêt, néanmoins aussi lourds peut-être à supporter que d'autres pour lesquels il y a de la sympathie.   (113)

Pour s'entendre entre mari et femme, entre collègues, entre amis, avec n'importe qui, entre les peuples, aux conférences de paix il ne d[oit] y avoir que ce moyen: le silence.   (117)

Les hommes ayant manqué de charité, la loi [a] dû leur en faire une stricte obligation. La pénible contrainte représent[e] donc une sorte de progrès en ce monde.   (123)

Les hommes et les femmes sur terre [sont] irrémédiablement isolés les uns des autres par les misères particulières à leur sexe et qu'à tout prendre celles des femmes [sont] peut-être les plus lourdes. (127)

☆   A sa manière, rien n'[est] plus injuste que la science.   (129)

Le malheur paraît alléger le poids familier de la vie.   (129)

La petite joie des autres, procurée à si bon compte, nous est quelquefois un reproche cuisant.   (131)

Mais lancé sur cette piste [la lecture de livres], on rencontre des bribes, des aspects de soi, partout.   (143)

☆   Tant de gens sur terre n'arrivent à exprimer leur affection que par l'inquiétude.   (150)

☆   Le meilleur du cœur semble destiné à s'user en regrets, à se perdre comme les ruisseaux, les sources, les rivières, toute l'eau vive et fraîche de la terre dans l'amertume de l'océan.   (151)

Si je n'ai rien à gagner, je n'ai rien à perdre.   (152)

Dans le vocabulaire des médecins tout est technique, et jusqu'aux secrets les plus craintifs de la vie.   (158)

Tant que la souffrance ser[a], admettr[a]-t-elle jamais de vie personnelle?   (170)

☆   Cette sorte de brusquerie qui t[ient] lieu de charité.   (172)

Peut-être ne devrait-on pas répéter aux gens qu'ils ont le droit d'être heureux. La permission pourrait mener un jour à une curieuse confusion.   (181)

Toutefois il arrive au hasard de la vie que des achats extravagants se révèlent économiques et qu'on ait lieu de se féliciter cent fois d'avoir commis au moins une folie.   (186)

☆   Ce point du voyage où ce que l'on éprouve n'est pas encore une illusion de recommencement mais bien plutôt une fin.   (196)

La solitude[:] absence de tout: des hommes, du passé, de l'avenir, du malheur, du bonheur; complet dépouillement.   (204)

Au matin, la solitude parl[e] le langage consolant de l'indifférence.   (205)

Oh, l'incomparable détachement du dormeur!

Qui donc n'a éprouvé que le sommeil dit la vérité sur nous. L'être humain y est enfin rendu à lui-même, ayant pris congé de tout le reste. Pieds et poings liés, ligoté par la fatigue, il coule enfin vers les cavernes de l'inconnu.   (210)

Certains hommes en sont remontés avec des poèmes tout faits; ou des équations résolues.   (210–11)

☆   Par le sommeil Dieu consentait que sa créature arrivât de temps en temps à se croire indépendante.   (211)

Et si c'était tout simplement pour ne plus voir souffrir la moitié du temps que Dieu avait décidé de ce tour de la terre autour du soleil?   (211)

Quelques hommes, lorsqu'on leur demande de préciser les jours où ils ont été heureux, peuvent hésiter entre trois ou quatre.   (213)

Un de ces poêles dont on connaît en les regardant qu'ils ont bien des nuits réchauffé un homme et ses pensées.   (216)

La moindre invention, à commencer par le seau témoign[e] ici de la fraternité.   (221)

☆   En vérité, la découverte du monde par un homme appuyé sur des siècles et des siècles de civilisation éblouit le cœur.   (221)

Ma cabane, mon lac, mon Dieu.   (222)

Ce d[oit] être en effet, … à la chaleur du feu qu'avait commençait de fondre la dureté des hommes.   (223)

☆   Que d'impressions heureuses en un seul jour peuvent donc pénétrer un cœur humain, lorsqu'il est libre de les accueillir!   (224)

On est toujours mieux à deux pour être content. Même un chien connaît cela.   (226)

[On est] redevable à des milliers d'hommes, et même à des morts.   (250)

La célérité avec laquelle il faut capter les pensées qui méritent d'être retenues.   (253)

☆   Il y aurait un abîme entre le bonheur de recevoir des autres [la beauté du monde] et celui d'en être soi-même l'instrument.   (255)

Au fond, de quoi l'homme heureux rend[…]-il grâce sinon de l'inégalité sur terre?   (258)

Pourquoi cette … fébrile curiosité pour les désastres?   (269)

Le salut [paraît] invraisemblable, une solution individuelle, toute solitaire au bout d'une promiscuité torturante.   (272)

☆   Ce siècle [est] bon pour les hommes, qui tiennent presque tous, d'abord, à vivre longtemps; ensuite, si possible, heureux.   (279)

☆   Les petites souffrances quotidiennes ne sont-elles pas, presque toujours, la garantie d'une longue vie?   (281)

Mais Dieu avait-il ratifié l'accord de Yalta?   (286)

S'ils était moins sûrs du ciel, est-ce que les hommes ne se mettraient pas plus sérieusement à leur tâche sur terre?   (286)

Mourir de faim n'[est] pas à la portée de tous.   (289)

Allez: il n'y a rien comme d'être mal portant pour apprécier la vie.

Il faut souffrir pour comprendre; et, comprendre, n'est-ce pas la plus grande richesse?

Dieu a bien fait son monde.   (291)

Sans doute, Dieu connaissait la souffrance des hommes en partie. Mais savait-il ce que c'était que de souffrir sans noblesse? De souffrir bêtement, petitement?   (294)

Une justice si complète que plus personne au monde ne serait heureux!   (297)

Quelquefois on a l'impression de s'entretenir avec un homme qui paraît presque au-delà de la vie. Cela porte à baisser le ton, à plus d'égards aussi.   (298)

En français, en anglais, toujours, il faut bien, car on est dans une ville [Montréal] qui pense et souffre en deux langues.   (308)

Pourquoi prie-t-on avec cet accent ennuyeux qui ravage le cœur d'inquiétude? Il semblerait alors qu'on s'adresse, sans beaucoup d'espoir d'être entendu, à quelqu'un de dur.   (312)

Mais, à ce passage de l'existence à la mort, est-ce qu'il y [a] lieu de s'enorgueillir des entreprises des autres?   (314)

Et où donc dans le monde y a-t-il plus de solidarité humaine que dans une banque?   (316)

☆   Il est des prêtres qui sont venus à Dieu par une ardente compassion pour l'homme; il en est d'autres pour qui les hommes ne seront jamais supportables qu'à cause de Dieu. Aux âmes sensibles, cette nuance est toujours perceptible.   (321)

☆   L'amour de Dieu suscit[e] chez l'homme d'église des pénitents assez dures, des actes de charité continuels, mais jamais – comment cela lui [peut-il être] possible? – un mouvement de tendre préférence en faveur de son pénitent.   (321–2)

Ces prêtres qui, plutôt qu'en alliés de Dieu se posent comme la police de Dieu; qui paraissent moins être du côté de Dieu qu'avoir Dieu de leur côté.   (322)

☆   Combien triste est l'amour au confessionnal!   (325)

Et combien d'hommes, s'ils avaient eu la possibilité comme Jésus de racheter les autres par leur mort, n'eussent pas longtemps hésité. Mourir sans profit pour personne, là [est] la véritable passion.   (327)

Dieu doit être très peu aimé pour lui-même, en effet, mais presque toujours par intérêt, puisqu'il dispos[e] de l'éternité.   (329)

[Dieu:] si difficile, sans égal, comment p[eut]-il ne pas être éternellement seul!   (329)

La drogue [... avec] son pouvoir dissolvant ... n'est-elle pas, hors la douleur, le plus énigmatique cadeau fait par Dieu aux hommes? (341–2)

☆   La ruse naturelle à l'homme qui juge à propos de demander un peu plus qu'il n'espère en réalité.   (344)

Et pourquoi Dieu avait-il créé la terre si belle puisque c'était pour lui soustraire les hommes?   (351)

Comment se fait-il que l'homme ayant conçu des supplices si précis pour se représenter l'enfer soit incapable, pour son bonheur, d'imaginer autre chose qu'une espèce de pompeux ennui! (352–3)

Mais alors, si Dieu pouvait faire une chose si difficile, pourquoi n'accordait-il pas aux hommes ce qu'ils désiraient plus encore que la résurrection des corps, c'est-à-dire de s'entendre entre eux, tels qu'ils étaient? (354)

Dans le monde organisé tel qu'il était, mourir rest[e] peut-être l'unique occasion de poser un geste d'absolue sincérité. (355)

Le vieux débat, si inutile …: Ce qu'on aurait pu être, certes c'[est] l'hypothèse entre toutes séduisantes – sans doute le rêve le plus captivant auquel un homme puisse se laisser aller. (361)

Les ingrates qualités qui ne rend[ent] pas nécessairement la vie facile, bien au contraire: la prudence, l'économie, l'honnêteté et, surtout, la redoutable franchise. (362)

Un être beaucoup plus mystérieux, presque un étranger; en quelque sorte un homme qui aurait pu être. (362)

"Voyez les lis des champs et les oiseaux." Très bien, mais ni les oiseaux mangeurs d'insectes, ni les lis abreuvés d'eau de pluie n'avaient à prévoir leur propre enterrement. (364)

Mieux employé, l'argent eût peut-être réussi à rendre les hommes presque heureux. (367)

Pauvre vie soucieuse de décorum. (367)

Où donc et de quelle manière la vie [a]-t-elle commencé d'être si extraordinairement faussée? Maintenant, d'erreur en erreur, elle était si absurdement déviée qu'il sembl[e] impossible d'entrevoir la cause initiale du mal. (368)

Si Dieu avait autant de cœur qu'un homme, déjà ce serait beau … très beau. (369)

Partir d'un pauvre cœur d'homme, d'une pauvre intelligence humaine pour imaginer Dieu, c'est de la folie! (370)

Sur terre, c'est ce qu'on fait; on tue le cœur des autres. (374)

☆   Cette longue et vraie connaissance des autres qui ne nous vient qu'à travers la peine. (377)

Le sort de la plupart des hommes qui est de rester enchaîné à l'insignifiance de la vie: vendre des chaussures pendant trente ans, être percepteur d'impôts. (381)

☆   Jusqu'où peut donc aller la délicatesse des hommes! (384)

c *Gouverneurs de la rosée*

Nous mourrons tous … (11)

Il y a si tellement beaucoup de pauvres créatures qui hèlent le bon Dieu de tout leur courage que ça fait un grand bruit ennuyant et le bon Dieu l'entend et il crie: Quel est, foutre, tout ce bruit? Et il bouche les oreilles. C'est la vérité et l'homme est abandonné. (11)

Le malheur bouleverse comme la bile, ça remonte à la bouche et alors les paroles sont amères. (12)

Un arbre, c'est fait pour vivre en paix dans la couleur du jour et l'amitié du soleil, du vent, de la pluie. (18)

Dans le corps c'est ce qu'il y a de plus récalcitrant, les reins. (19)

Si l'on est d'un pays, si l'on y est né, comme qui dirait: natif-natal, eh bien, on l'a dans les yeux, la peau, les mains, avec la chevelure de ses arbres, la chair de sa terre, les os de ses pierres, le sang de ses rivières, son ciel, sa saveur, ses hommes et ses femmes: c'est une présence, dans le cœur, source de son regard, le fruit de sa bouche, les collines de ses seins, ses mains qui se défendent et se rendent, ses genoux sans mystères, sa force et sa faiblesse, sa voix et son silence. (26)

Ce n'est pas si tellement le temps qui fait l'âge, c'est les tribulations de l'existence. (29)

La rage te fait serrer les mâchoires et boucler ta ceinture plus près de la peau de ton ventre quand tu as faim. La rage c'est une grande force. (29)

C'est comme ça: il n'y a pas de consolation. (29)

– En vérité, il y a une consolation, je vais te dire: c'est la terre, ton morceau de terre fait pour le courage de tes bras, avec tes arbres fruitiers à l'entour, tes bêtes dans le pâturage, toutes tes nécessités à portée de la main et ta liberté qui n'a pas une autre limite que la saison bonne ou mauvaise, la pluie ou la sécheresse. (29–30)

La vie, c'est la vie: tu as beau prendre des chemins de traverse, faire un long détour, la vie c'est un retour continuel. (34)

Le fruit pourrit dans la terre et nourrit l'espoir de l'arbre nouveau. (34)

Il y a les affaires du ciel et il y a les affaires de la terre: ça fait deux et ce n'est pas la même chose. Le ciel, c'est le pâturage des anges; ils sont bienheureux; ils n'ont pas à prendre soin du manger et du boire. Et sûrement qu'il y a des anges nègres pour faire le gros travail de la lessive des nuages ou balayer la pluie et mettre la propreté du soleil après l'orage, pendant que les anges blancs chantent comme des rossignols toute la sainte journée ou bien soufflent dans de petites trompettes comme c'est marqué dans les images qu'on voit dans les églises.

Mais la terre, c'est une bataille jour pour jour, une bataille sans repos: défricher, planter, sarcler, arroser, jusqu'à la récolte, et alors tu vois ton champ mûr couché devant toi le matin, sous la rosée, et l'orgueil entre dans ton cœur. Mais la terre est comme une bonne femme, à force de la maltraiter, elle se révolte: j'ai vu que vous avez déboisé les mornes. La terre est toute nue et sans protection. Ce sont les racines qui font amitié avec la terre et la retiennent; ce sont les manguiers, les bois de chênes, les acajous qui lui donnent les eaux des pluies pour sa grande soif et leur ombrage contre la chaleur de midi. C'est comme ça et pas autrement, sinon la pluie écorche la terre et le soleil l'échaude: il ne reste plus que les roches. (37)

C'est pas Dieu qui abandonne le nègre, c'est le nègre qui abandonne la terre et il reçoit sa punition: la sécheresse, la misère et la désolation. (37)

Mais il n'y a pas de miséricorde pour les malheureux. (47)

C'est traître, la résignation; c'est du pareil au même que le découragement. Ça vous casse les bras: on attend les miracles et la Providence, chapelet en main, sans rien faire. On prie pour la pluie, on prie pour la récolte, on dit les oraisons des saints et des loa [divinités afro-haïtiennes]. Mais la Providence, laisse-moi te dire, c'est le propre vouloir du nègre de ne pas accepter le malheur, de dompter chaque jour la mauvaise volonté de la terre, de soumettre le caprice de l'eau à ses besoins; alors la terre l'appelle: cher maître, et l'eau l'appelle: cher maître, et il n'y a d'autre Providence que son travail d'habitant sérieux, d'autre miracle que le fruit de ses mains. (47)

L'ignorance et le besoin marchent ensemble, pas vrai?   (52)

Ne commence pas avec les compliments, ça ne sert à rien et ce n'est pas nécessaire.   (82)

L'expérience est le bâton des aveugles ... et ce qui compte, ... c'est la rébellion, et la connaissance que l'homme est le boulanger de la vie.   (84)

La grève c'est ça: un NON de mille voix qui ne font qu'une et qui s'abat sur la table du patron avec le pesant d'une roche.   (86)

Tu vois, c'est la plus grande chose au monde que tous les hommes sont frères, qu'ils ont le même poids dans la balance de la misère et de l'injustice.   (87)

Et il y a des fois, tu sais, le cœur et la raison c'est du pareil au même.   (87)

Les femmes, c'est changeant comme le temps. Mais c'est un proverbe qui n'est pas vrai, parce que je voudrais bien, moi, qu'une bonne pluie tombe après toute cette sécheresse.   (98–9)

C'est l'existence qui leur a appris, aux négresses, à chanter comme on étouffe un sanglot et c'est une chanson qui finit toujours par un recommencement parce qu'elle est à l'image de la misère, et dites-moi, est-ce que ça finit jamais, la misère?   (99)

La vie est faite pour que les hommes, tous les nègres, aient leur satisfaction et leur contentement, ... un jour s'en va et un jour viendra qui apportera cette vérité, mais en attendant, la vie est une punition, voilà ce qu'elle est, la vie.   (99–100)

Et le bon Dieu va se fatiguer de t'entendre nommer son nom pour un oui et pour un non.   (101)

Retrouver l'amitié entre frères et refaire la vie comme elle doit être: un service de bonne volonté entre nègres pareils par la nécessité et la destinée.   (105)

Quand un homme commence à avoir du guignon, dit-on, même le lait caillé peut lui casser la tête.   (109)

Chaque nègre pendant son existence y fait un nœud: c'est le travail qu'il a accompli et c'est ça qui rend la vie vivante dans les siècles des siècles: l'utilité de l'homme sur cette terre.   (113)

Sans la concorde la vie n'a pas de goût, la vie n'a pas de sens.   (127)

On ne peut pas avaler une grappe de raisin d'un seul coup, mais grain par grain, c'est facile.   (126)

C'est rebelle à périr, le nègre. C'est dur comme pas un.   (131)

La menterie ... c'est comme de l'argent placé à l'intérêt. Faut que ça rapporte.   (134)

C'est la vie qui commande et quand la vie commande, faut répondre: présent.   (132)

Et si l'habitant allait à l'école, certain qu'on ne pourrait plus si facilement le tromper, l'abuser et le traiter en bourrique.   (150)

Parce que ce qui compte, c'est le sacrifice de l'homme. C'est le sang du nègre.   (160)

La vie, c'est une comédie, voilà ce qu'elle est la vie.   (164)

Le Bondieu est bon, dit-on. Le Bondieu est blanc, qu'il faudrait dire. Et peut-être que c'est tout juste le contraire.   (165)

On n'invite pas le malheur … Et il vient et il se met à table sans permission et il mange et ne laisse que les os.   (166)

L'église ne fait pas de crédit aux malheureux c'est pas une boutique, c'est la maison de Dieu.   (167)

À la fin on se fatigue même du chagrin.   (167)

Entre les larmes et le rire. Tout comme la vie, compère, oui tout juste comme la vie.   (173)

Ils sont endurants, les chanteurs de cantiques, ils ne s'essoufflent pas facilement.   (175)

Parce que ce qui compte, c'est le sacrifice de l'homme, le sang du nègre.   (185)

Du bon matériau d'habitants: simples, francs, honnêtes.   (186)

La vie c'est un fil qui ne se casse pas, qui ne se perd jamais et tu sais pourquoi? Parce que chaque nègre pendant son existence y fait un nœud: c'est le travail qu'il a accompli et c'est ça qui rend la vie vivante dans les siècles des siècles: l'utilité de l'homme sur cette terre.   (191)

Les plantes, c'est comme les chrétiens. Il y en a de deux qualités: les bonnes et les mauvaises. Quand tu vois des oranges, tous ces petits soleils accrochés dans le feuillage, tu sens comme une réjouissance, c'est plaisant et c'est serviable, les oranges. Tandis que, prends une plante à piquants comme celle-là … Mais, il ne faut rien maudire parce que c'est le bon Dieu qui a tout créé.   (191)

D *Pluie et vent sur Télumée Miracle*

Le pays dépend bien souvent du cœur de l'homme: il est minuscule si le cœur est petit, et immense si le cœur est grand. (11)

Ici comme partout ailleurs, rire et chanter, danser, rêver n'est pas exactement toute la réalité. (18)

Malheur à celui qui rit une fois et s'y habitue, car la scélératesse de la vie est sans limites et lorsqu'elle vous comble d'une main, c'est pour vous piétiner des deux pieds, lancer à vos trousses cette femme folle, la déveine, qui vous happe et vous déchire et voltige les lambeaux de votre chair aux corbeaux. (23)

Face au mensonge des choses, à la tristesse, il y a et il y aura toujours la fantaisie de l'homme. (25)

Le mal des humains est grand et peut faire d'un homme n'importe quoi, même un assassin, messieurs, c'est pas une blague, un assassin. (40)

La vérité est qu'un rien, une idée, une lubie, un grain de poussière suffisent à changer le cours d'une vie. (46)

Trois sentiers sont mauvais pour l'homme: voir la beauté du monde, et dire qu'il est laid, se lever de grand matin pour faire ce dont on est incapable, et donner libre cours à ses songes, sans se surveiller, car qui songe devient victime de son propre songe. (51)

Si votre cœur est bien monté, vous voyez la vie comme on doit la voir, avec la même humeur qu'un brave en équilibre sur une boule et qui va tomber, mais il durera le plus longtemps possible, voilà. (77)

Maintenant écoutez autre chose: les biens de la terre restent à la terre, et l'homme ne possède même pas la peau qui l'enveloppe. Tout ce qu'il possède: les sentiments de son cœur.   (77)

Si grand que soit le mal, l'homme doit se faire encore plus grand, dût-il s'ajuster des échasses.   (79)

Derrière une peine il y a une autre peine, la misère est une vague sans fin, mais le cheval ne doit pas te conduire, c'est toi qui dois conduire le cheval.   (79)

On peut prendre méandre sur méandre, tourner, contourner, s'insinuer dans la terre, vos méandres vous appartiennent mais la vie est là, patiente, sans commencement et sans fin, à vous attendre, pareille à l'océan.   (81)

Une feuille tombe et la forêt entière frémit.   (109)

Il y a l'air, l'eau, le ciel et la terre sur laquelle on marche, et l'amour. C'est ce qui nous fait vivre.   (115)

Tout dépend du vent, il y en a qui vous font tomber, et d'autres qui raffermissent vos attaches, vous fortifient.   (118)

Bienheureux celui qui navigue dans l'incertitude, qui ne sait ce qu'il a semé, ni ce qu'il va récolter.   (132)

Danser trop tôt n'est pas danser.   (136)

Tu as le devoir aujourd'hui de te réjouir sans appréhension ni retenue.   (137)

Il faut stopper le mal par notre silence et d'ailleurs, depuis quand la misère est-elle un conte?   (144)

Ami, rien ne poursuit le nègre que son propre cœur.   (147)

La femme qui rit est celle-là même qui va pleurer, et c'est pourquoi on sait déjà, à la façon dont une femme est heureuse quel maintien elle aura devant l'adversité.   (153)

Il me restait bien des découvertes à faire avant que je sache ce que signifie exactement cela: *être une femme sur la terre.*   (159, emphasis added)

Le soleil n'est jamais fatigué de se lever, mais il arrive que l'homme soit las de se retrouver sous le soleil.   (166)

Voir tant de misères, recevoir tant de crachats, devenir impotent et mourir … la vie sur terre convient-elle donc vraiment à l'homme? (179)

L'homme n'est pas un nuage au vent que la mort dissipe et efface d'un seul coup.   (183)

L'homme n'est qu'un poisson qui mange de l'homme.   (218)

La vie est une mer sans escale, sans phare aucun … et les hommes sont des navires sans destination.   (247–8)

E *La Route des Flandres*

Il y a des choses que le pire des abandons des renoncements ne peut faire oublier même si on le voulait et ce sont en général les plus absurdes les plus vides de sens celles qui ne se raisonnent ni se commandent. (12)

Il est inévitable de rencontrer toujours partout et en toutes circonstances – dans les salons ou à la guerre – des gens stupides et sans éducation. (18)

Le temps n'existe pas. (19)

Le cheminement même du temps, c'est-à-dire invisible immatériel sans commencement ni fin ni repère. (28)

Cette irrésistible lenteur de tout ce qui de près ou de loin et de quelque espèce que ce soit – hommes, animaux, mécaniques – touche aux choses de la terre. (32)

Ce comment s'appelait-il philosophe qui a dit que l'homme ne connaissait que deux moyens de s'approprier ce qui appartient aux autres, la guerre et le commerce, et qu'il choisissait en général tout d'abord le premier parce qu'il lui paraissait le plus facile et le plus rapide et ensuite, mais seulement après avoir découvert les inconvénients et les dangers du premier, le second c'est-à-dire le commerce qui était un moyen non moins déloyal et brutal mais plus confortable, et qu'au demeurant tous les peuples étaient obligatoirement passés par ces deux phases et avaient chacun à son tour mis l'Europe à feu et à sang avant de se transformer en sociétés anonymes de commis-voyageur comme les Anglais mais que guerre et commerce n'étaient jamais l'un comme l'autre que l'expression de leur rapacité elle-même la conséquence de l'ancestrale terreur de la faim et de la mort, ce qui faisait que tuer voler piller et vendre n'étaient en réalité qu'une seule et même chose un simple besoin celui de se rassurer, comme des gamins qui sifflent et chantent fort pour se donner du courage en traversant une forêt la nuit.   (33–4)

Cette pesante obstinée et superstitieuse crédulité – ou plutôt croyance – en l'absolue prééminence du savoir appris par procuration, de ce qui est écrit.   (34–5)

Cet attachement hautain du maître pour son chien et de bas en haut du chien pour son maître.   (43)

À moins que, justement, l'amour – ou plutôt la passion – ce soit cela: cette chose muette, ces élans, ces répulsions, ces haines, tout informulé – et même informé –, et donc cette simple suite de gestes, de paroles de scènes insignifiantes, et, au centre, sans préambule, cet assaut, ce corps-à-corps urgent, rapide sauvage n'importe où.   (48–9)

Le temps supprimé, comme l'épiderme même des ambitions, des rêves, des vanités, des futiles et impérissables passions.   (52)

Un groupe d'hommes gesticulant, s'échauffant, s'affrontant, les voix se mêlant en une sorte de chœur incohérent, désordonné, de babelesque criaillerie, comme sous le poids d'une malédiction, une parodie de ce langage qui, avec l'inflexible perfidie des choses créées ou asservies par l'homme, se retournent contre lui et se vengent avec d'autant plus de traîtrise et d'efficacité qu'elles semblent apparemment remplir docilement leur fonction: obstacle majeur, donc, à toute communication, toute compréhension.   (56–7)

Les lointaines et inaltérables étoiles stagnant, immobiles, virginales, apparaissant et disparaissant dans les découpures qui s'ouvrent et se referment entre les têtes, comme une surface glacée, cristalline et inviolable sur laquelle pouvait glisser sans laisser ni trace ni souillure cette matière noirâtre, visqueuse vociférante et moite d'où émanaient les voix à présent plaintives et furieuses pour de bon.   (67)

Cet air un peu niais, surpris, incrédule et doux qu'ont ceux des gens tués de mort violente, comme si au dernier moment leur avait été révélé quelque chose à quoi durant toute leur vie ils n'avaient jamais eu l'idée de penser, c'est-à-dire sans doute quelque chose d'absolument contraire à ce que peut apprendre la pensée, de tellement étonnant, de tellement.   (70)

Le point critique où l'esprit (pas le corps, qui peut en supporter beaucoup plus) ne peut plus endurer une minute de plus l'idée – le supplice – de posséder quelque chose qui peut être mangé.   (71)

Comme toute mascarade – vaguement pédérastique.   (75)

Cette expression ahurie stupéfaite comme par la brusque révélation de la mort c'est-à-dire enfin connue non plus sous la forme abstraite de ce concept avec lequel nous avons pris l'habitude de vivre mais surgie ou plutôt frappant dans sa réalité physique, cette violence cette agression, un coup injuste imméritée la fureur stupide et stupéfiante des choses qui n'ont pas besoin de raison pour frapper comme quand on se cogne la tête la première dans un réverbère qu'on n'avait pas vu perdu dans ses pensées.   (83–4)

Parce que comment peut-on dire depuis combien de temps un homme est mort puisque pour lui hier tout à l'heure et demain ont définitivement cessé d'exister c'est-à-dire de le préoccuper c'est-à-dire de l'embêter.   (99)

En définitive l'idiotie ou l'intelligence n'avaient pas grand'chose à voir dans tout cela je veux dire avec nous je veux dire avec ce que nous croyons être nous et qui nous fait parler agir haïr aimer puisque, cela parti, notre corps notre visage continue à exprimer ce que nous nous figurions être propre à notre esprit alors peut-être ces choses je veux dire l'intelli-gence l'idiotie ou être amoureux ou brave ou lâche ou meurtrier les qualités les passions existent-elles en dehors de nous venant se loger sans nous demander notre avis dans cette grossière carcasse qu'elles possèdent.   (111)

Un homme peut arriver à se faire croire à peu près n'importe quoi pourvu que ça l'arrange.   (112)

Cette virginité ces désirs virginaux.   (114)

Ce bouillonnement caché des passions.   (115)

Cette fausse insouciance, cette fausse gaieté, ce faux cynisme des jeunes gens.   (120)

À part la certitude de crever qu'est-ce qu'il y a de plus réel? ... la certitude qu'il faut bouffer.   (123)

Ces objets parmi lesquels il rangeait sans doute les vedettes de cinéma (privées de toute réalité, sauf féerique), les chevaux, ou encore ces choses (montagnes, bateaux, avions, auxquelles l'homme qui per-çoit par leur intermédiaire les manifestations des forces naturelles contre lesquelles il lutte, attribue des réactions (colère, méchanceté, traîtrise) humaines: êtres (les chevaux, les déesses sur celluloïd, les autos) d'une nature hybride, ambiguë, pas tout à fait humains, pas tout à fait objets, inspirant à la fois le respect et l'irrespect par la rencontre, la réunion en eux d'éléments composants (réels ou suppo-sés) disparates – humains et inhumains.   (132–3)

L'expérience intime, atavique, passée au stade du réflexe, de la stupidité et de la méchanceté humaines.   (159)

Le logique aboutissement d'ordres, de dispositions peut-être rationnelles à l'origine, et démentielles au stade de l'exécution, comme chaque fois qu'un mécanisme d'exécution suffisamment rigide, comme l'armée, ou rapide, comme les révolutions, renvoie à l'homme sans ces retouches, cet assouplissement qu'apportent soit une application infidèle, soit le temps, le reflet exact de sa pensée nue. (161)

Cette faiblesse que ne connaissent pas les loups mais seulement les hommes, c'est-à-dire la raison. (162)

Cette totale absence de sens moral ou de charité dont sont seulement capables les enfants, cette candide cruauté inhérente à la nature même de l'enfance (l'orgueilleux, l'impétueux et irrépressible bouillonnement de la vie). (166)

Faire surgir les images châtoyantes et lumineuses au moyen de l'éphémère, l'incantatoire magie du langage, des mots inventés dans l'espoir de rendre comestible – comme ces pâtes vaguement sucrées sous lesquelles on dissimule aux enfants les médicaments amers – l'innommable réalité. (173)

Cette forme futile et illusoire de la vie qu'est le mouvement (le temps de parcourir à son tour une dizaine ou une quinzaine de mètres). (231)

Les gens aiment tellement faire de la tragédie du drame du roman. (262)

Comme ça doit être chouette d'avoir tellement de temps à sa disposition que le suicide, le drame, la tragédie deviennent des sortes d'élégants passe-temps. (268)

Mais comment appeler cela: non pas la guerre non pas la classique destruction ou extermination d'une des deux armées mais plutôt la disparition l'absorption par le néant ou le tout originel de qui une semaine auparavant était encore des régiment des batteries des escadrons des escouades des hommes, ou plus encore: la disparition de l'idée de la notion même de régiment de batterie d'escadron d'escouade de l'homme, ou plus encore: la disparition de toute idée de tout concept. (282)

Mais comment savoir, comment savoir? (285)

Un invisible et complexe réseau de forces d'impulsion d'attraction ou de répulsions d'attraction ou de répulsions s'entrecroisant et se combinant pour former pour ainsi dire par leurs résultante le polygone de sustentation du groupe se déformant lui-même sans cesse du fait des incessantes modifications provoquées par des accidents internes ou externes. (285)

Cet impérieux souci d'élégance. (286)

Cette hypothèque pratiquement impossible à lever que constitue entre deux êtres humains une énorme différence de disponibilités monétaires, puis de grades. (287)

Mais comment savoir, que savoir?   (289)

Cette espèce de néant comme on dit qu'au centre d'un typhon il existe une zone parfaitement calme de la connaissance, de point zéro.   (296)

Le monde arrêté figé s'effritant se dépiautant s'écroulant peu à peu par morceaux comme une bâtisse abandonné, inutilisable, livrée à l'incohérent, nonchalant, impersonnel et destructeur travail du temps.   (296)

F *Présence de la mort*

On n'a pas beaucoup d'imagination chez nous. (16)

Il faudrait pouvoir imaginer le ciel, les astres, les continents, les océans, l'équateur, les deux pôles. Or, on n'imagine rien que soi et ce qui est autour de soi. (18)

Les choses qu'on devra quitter, peut-être: ... les aimer davantage. Et connaître enfin l'espace, le généreux, le varié, le large et long, l'abondant, le très vaste, – dans sa solitude et sa nudité. (24)

Un homme comme ça, c'est-à-dire comme beaucoup d'autres, multipliant, additionnant, faisant des soustractions. (28)

Il y a plusieurs réalités. (30)

Et il y a l'amour. (31)

Il y a un amour qui prétend et un amour qui renonce. Il y a des amours contradictoires. Il y a des contradictions dans l'amour. (31)

Regarder ce qui est, et ne rien mettre ici que ce qui est. (34)

Défense de parler au conducteur: quand on ne lui parle pas, c'est lui qui vous parle. (38)

... or, c'est justement ce qui devrait vous rassurer qui vous inquiète. (39)

Car il y a ceux qui ont et ceux qui n'ont pas. (47)

La plupart des hommes sont ainsi faits qu'ils ne peuvent s'intéresser qu'à l'immédiat et au détail; ils aiment à se laisser tromper. Peu lèvent les yeux jusqu'au ciel, peu le comprennent. Peu savent même qu'il existe, et là-haut le grand mécanisme, l'astre plus ou moins proche, l'astre se rapprochant toujours. (48)

Le soleil prend à une place; à une autre, il donne. (50)

Le goût de la destruction vous vient pour la seule destruction. Avant même qu'on soit ivre de vin, car il n'y a pas que cette ivresse … Et il y a de même un travail plus beau que de faire, une plus belle espèce de travail: c'est de défaire. (70)

C'est ça qui est beau; – étant plusieurs, n'étant qu'une seule personne. (71)

Dans la simplicité et en même temps dans la vérité, parce qu'il est dans l'innocence. (75)

Salut! encore une fois, salut, toi d'abord, la réelle! Et salut, l'imaginée, celle que j'imagine encore, comme quand le potier fait son vase, l'ayant façonné, lui aussi, dans sa tête, puis faisant sortir peu à peu cette conception qu'il a, de la terre glaise, faisant descendre la forme depuis sa tête le long de ses bras jusqu'à ses doigts. (89)

Et salut! vite encore, parce que tu t'en vas, parce que tout s'en va, parce que rien ne doit durer, parce que rien ne peut durer, salut une dernière fois! (90)

Jusqu'au bout, jusqu'au tout dernier moment, tant que tu pourras; tant qu'un petit reste de souffle te sera accordé, un rien de souffle encore, parce que le mot est court (et peut-être bien est-ce pourquoi il est court). (94)

Comme on est seul pour mourir! Chaque chose, chaque être, seuls devant rien. (96)

On fait tout ce qu'on peut, on cherche à se défendre, même si ça ne doit servir à rien. (103)

On va à la mort par peur de la mort. C'est tellement incompréhensible! Voilà comment l'homme est fait, ce rien qui est tout, puis il n'est plus rien du tout. (107)

Nous sommes tellement balancés. Tellement portés, tout le temps, de l'une des extrémités de nous à l'autre extrémité. Qui sommes nous? Qui sommes nous? (120)

Des espèces de glaneurs en tout, n'étant des moissonneurs en rien. (140)

g *Neige noire*

Cette spécificité cinématographique est d'ailleurs infiniment séduisante: elle ressemble à l'aventure aléatoire de chaque individu. La vie ne permet pas d'aller bien loin, non plus que d'approfondir le sens de tout ce qui est. L'être humain, si doué soit-il, reste toujours à l'extérieur de ce qu'il veut percer. (28)

Trouver une métaphore filmique du bonheur. Des plans obliques des yeux ou des profils à contre-jour. Il importe de ne pas charger, car la béatitude ne se mesure pas à l'intensité. (40)

(Une succession n'est jamais finie. A sa passation est rattachée l'inéluctable opération suivante: une autre succession. Et cela continue, se reproduit, recommence, n'arrête qu'un temps pour reprendre à nouveau et ainsi de suite. Ce qui se succède finit immanquablement par obséder. Personne n'est immunisé contre la dissolution du temps. Même le sommeil n'a jamais endigué les eaux sauvages du ressouvenir.) (48)

L'écriture altère le mouvement de la vie, tandis que le cinéma, moins précis dans la description, rend ce qui est le plus précieux chez les êtres qu'il représente: le mouvement. (51)

La discontinuité présuppose la continuité. (53)

En vérité, le cours de la vie est chaotique et imprévisible. (54)

Les désignations de la réalité n'ajoutent rien à la réalité, sinon un masque nominal. (62)

Le temps ne s'arrête pas, non! Le temps ne s'arrêtera plus: il supprime, par le vide, tout ce qui le précède et tout ce qui le suivra. (69–70)

Plus on aime, plus on devient injuste, quelle étrange loi! (79)

Toute représentation de l'irreprésentable est forcément sujette à des coups de théâtre improvisés. (91)

Le temps déporte tout selon un diagramme toujours pareil, connu de tous et pourtant difficile parfois à réinventer par le seul jeu de la mémoire. On ne feuillette pas le temps, c'est lui qui effeuille nos vies. (125)

Oui, le temps transitif coule selon une transience frénatrice, alors que l'autre, le temps immanent de la joie et de l'amour, se définit comme l'haleine de la beauté. (127)

Si le silence a une couleur, il est noir. (132)

Je n'étais pas, j'ai été, je me souviens, je ne suis plus. (138)

Le Québec est en creux. Son éclipse récurrente fait penser à l'absence d'une présence, à un mystère inachevé. (143)

Rien n'est plus corrosif que le doute. (153)

L'autobiographique est une fausse catégorie. (154)

La fiction n'est pas un piège, c'est elle, plutôt, qui est piégée par une réalité qu'elle ne contenait pas et qui l'envahit hypocritement. (155)

Le temps est une vierge enceinte. Et si c'est un fleuve, ce fleuve est un cimetière rapide qui emporte tout, même les berges qui l'étreignent, les arbres qui le bordent et les barques qu'il porte! Le film, mieux que tout autre moyen d'expression, rend bien cette fluidité achérontique, dans la mesure au moins où il ne s'arrête jamais avant la fin de sa propre projection … Donc, vingt-quatre images par seconde réussissent pour que le spectateur n'aperçoive ni les rivets, ni les collures, ni les pales de l'obturateur. Cette poudre nyctalope s'introduit dans le cerveau du spectateur et lui permet de reconstituer le fleuve temporaire qui nous conduit tous à la mort. (157)

Quelque chose de difficile à avouer est lié à toute obscurité librement consentie, fût-ce celle d'un cinéma, et, pour cette raison même, les gens devraient aller au cinéma masqués. (167)

La vie est probablement trop courte pour qu'on se tienne au courant des plus récentes techniques d'abduction, il suffit d'être enlevé. Mieux encore: il suffit de vouloir partir. (174)

Car la beauté aura le pouvoir de réduire l'honnêteté en maquerelle, bien plutôt que l'honnêteté d'élever jusqu'à soi la beauté. (176, *mise en abyme* from *Hamlet*)

La seule façon que l'humanité a trouvée de dominer le temps, c'est de le spatialiser *ad nauseam*. (194)

L'amour, si délibérément intrusif soit-il, se ramène à une approximation vélaire de l'autre, à une croisière désespérante sur le toit d'une mer qu'on ne peut jamais percer. (195)

Les dialogues qui sonnent un peu faux ont, plus que les conversations réalistes, le pouvoir de rendre le fantastique.   (199)

La parole engendre, elle ne fait pas qu'orner ou accompagner l'existence.   (199)

Mais ce qui cesse pourrait continuer et ce qui continue avait donc cessé; reprendre, c'est postuler l'arrêt antérieur, la brisure provisoire. (205)

La fiction, plus large que la vérité parce qu'indéterminée, englobe accidentellement la vérité.   (230)

Les livres se ferment et s'ouvrent sans douleur, sans problème, tout au plus avec un petit craquement de l'épine. De plus, ils ne voient rien; ce sont des objets aveugles comme leurs auteurs.   (235–6)

(On emploie le présent pour faire l'inventaire de ce qui manque. Ce présent tabulaire évoque des lacunes, des creux, des omissions des absences.)   (241)

Comme dans la musique, il n'y a jamais de reprise identique; quand les corps s'unissent à nouveau, la mémoire des étreintes qui ont précédé est anéantie par l'émotion nouvelle. Tout reprend parce que tout finit; et cette mélodie qui ne se ressemble jamais tout à fait nous rapproche d'une étreinte finale qui abolit tout.)   (244)

L'amour donne le vertige, mais son vertige, si intolérable qu'il soit, est un délice infini.   (264)

Enfuyons-nous vers notre seule patrie! Que la vie plénifiante qui a tissé ces fibrilles, ces rubans arciformes, ces ailes blanches de l'âme, continue éternellement vers le point oméga que l'on n'atteint qu'en mourant et en perdant toute identité, pour renaître et vivre dans le Christ de la Révélation.   (264)

References

Aquin, Hubert. *Prochain épisode*. Ottawa: Le Cercle du Livre de France 1965.
- *Neige noire*. 1974. Montréal: Pierre Tisseyre 1978.
- "La Disparition élocutoire du poète." In *Blocs erratiques*. Montréal: Stanké 1982. 263–7.
Barthes, Roland. *Le Degré zéro de l'écriture*. 1953. Paris: Editions du Seuil 1972.
Becker, A.L. "Text-building, Epistemology, and Esthetics in Javanese Shadow Theater." In *The Imagination of Reality*, ed. A.L. Becker and A.A. Yengoyan. Norwood, NJ: Ablex 1979. 211–43.
Bennington, Geoffrey. *Sententiousness and the Novel: Laying Down the Law in Eighteenth-Century French Fiction*. Cambridge: Cambridge University Press 1985.
Beutel, August Wilhelm. *"Der Aphorismus": Lärchenflügelschläge*. Essen: Verlag Die Blaue Eule 1988.
Bevan, David. *Charles-Ferdinand Ramuz*. Boston: Twayne Publishers 1979.
Biyidi, O. "Simone Schwarz-Bart." In *Dictionnaire de littératures de langue française*, ed. J.-P. Beaumarchais, Daniel Couty, and Alain Rey. Paris: Bordas 1984. 2147–8.
Burke, Kenneth. "Literature as Equipment for Living." In *The Philosophy of Literary Form*. New York: Vantage Books 1967. 293–304.
Camus, Albert. *La Peste*. Paris: Gallimard 1947.
Chevrier, Pierre. *Antoine de Saint-Exupéry*. Paris: Gallimard 1949.
Clive, Geoffrey. *The Philosophy of Nietzsche*. New York: New American Library 1965.
Colette. *La Naissance du jour*. 1928. Paris: Flammarion 1984.
Dällenbach, Lucien. *Claude Simon*. Paris: Editions du Seuil 1988.

Delson-Karan, Myrna. "The Last Interview." *Québec Studies* 4 (1986): 198–9.

Ducrot, Oswald, and Tzvetan Todorov. *Encyclopedic Dictionary of the Sciences of Language*. Trans. Catherine Porter. 1972. Baltimore: Johns Hopkins University Press 1979.

Estang, Luc. *Saint-Exupéry*. Paris: Editions du Seuil 1956.

Fowler, Carolyn. *A Knot in the Thread: The Life and Work of Jacques Roumain*. Washington, DC: Howard University Press 1980.

Fowler, Roger. *Linguistics and the Novel*. London and New York: Methuen 1977.

Fricke, Harald. *Aphorismus*. Stuttgart: Metzler 1984.

Gide, André. *L'Immoraliste*. 1902. London: Harrap 1974.

Gray, Richard T. *Constructive Deconstruction*. Tübingen: Max Niemeyer Verlag 1987.

Gross, John, ed. *The Oxford Book of Aphorisms*. Oxford: Oxford University Press 1987.

Hébert, Anne. *Kamouraska*. Paris: Editions du Seuil 1971.

Heidenreich, Rosmarin. *The Postwar Novel in Canada*. Waterloo, Ont.: Wilfrid Laurier University Press 1989.

Hopper, Paul. "Aspect and Foregrounding in Discourse." In *Syntax and Semantics: Discourse and Syntax*, vol. 12, ed. T. Given. New York: Academic Press 1979. 213–41.

Humphries, Jefferson. *The Puritan and the Cynic*. New York and Oxford: Oxford University Press 1987.

Jiménez-Fajardo, Salvador. *Claude Simon*. Boston: Twayne Publishers 1975.

Kadish, Doris Y. *Practices of the New Novel in Claude Simon's "L'Herbe" and "La Route des Flandres"*. Fredericton, NB: York Press 1979.

Kruger, Heinz. *Über den Aphorismus als Philosophische Form*. 1957. München: Edition Text + Kritik 1988.

Labov, William. "The Transformation of Experience in Narrative Syntax." In *Language and the Inner City*. Philadelphia: University of Pennsylvania Press 1972. 354–96.

La Rochefoucault. *Maximes*. 1665. Cambridge: Cambridge University Press 1945.

Marcel, Jean. *Rina Lasnier*. Ottawa: Fides 1964.

May, Cedric. Review of *Hubert Aquin dix ans après*. *British Journal of Canadian Studies* 3 (1988): 388.

Montaigne. Essais. 1580. Livre premier (extraits). Paris: Larousse, 1965.

Nelligan, Emile. *Poèmes choisis*. Montréal: Fides 1983.

Nietzsche, Friedrich. *Werke in drei Bänden*. Ed. Karl Schlechta. München: Carl Hanser Verlag 1965.

Ormerod, Beverley. *An Introduction to the French Caribbean Novel*. London: Heinemann 1985.

Ouellet, Réal. *Les Relations humaines dans l'œuvre de Saint-Exupéry*. Paris: Minard 1971.

Pascal, Blaise. *Pensées*. 1670. Paris: Librairie Générale Française 1972.

Pélissier, Georges. *Les Cinq Visages de Saint-Exupéry.* Paris: Flammarion 1951.

Proust, Marcel. *Du Côté de chez Swann*. 1913. Paris: Gallimard 1954.

– *Le Temps retrouvé*. 1913. Paris: Gallimard 1954.

Rader, Margaret. "Context in Written Language: The Case of Imaginative Fiction." In *Spoken and Written Language: Exploring Orality and Literacy,* ed. Deborah Tannen. Norwook, NJ: Ablex 1982. 185–98.

Ramuz, Charles-Ferdinand. *Présence de la mort*. 1905. Lausanne: Editions de l'Aire 1978.

– *L'Exemple de Cézanne*. [1914.] Aigre: Editions Séquences 1988.

– "Taille de l'homme." 1933. In *La Pensée remonte les fleuves*. Paris: Librairie Plon 1979.

– *Derborence*. Paris: Grasset 1936.

Renault, Alain. *L'Ère de l'individu*. Paris: Gallimard 1989.

Ricoeur, Paul. *Hermeneutics and the Human Sciences*. Ed. and trans. John B. Thompson. 1981. Cambridge: Cambridge University Press and Edition de la Maison des Sciences de l'Homme 1989.

Robbe-Grillet, Alain. *La Jalousie*. Paris: Les Editions de Minuit 1957.

Roumain, Jacques. *Gouverneurs de la rosée*. 1946. Paris: Editions Messidor 1989.

Roy, Gabrielle. *Alexandre Chenevert*. 1954. Montréal: Stanké 1979.

Saint-Exupéry, Antoine de. *Terre des hommes*. Paris: Gallimard 1939.

– *Citadelle*. Paris: Gallimard 1948.

– *Carnets*. Paris: Gallimard 1975.

Sarraute, Nathalie. *Le Planétarium*. Paris: Gallimard 1959.

Sartre, Jean-Paul. *La Nausée*. Paris: Gallimard 1938.

Schwarz-Bart, Simone. *Pluie et vent sur Télumée Miracle*. Paris: Editions du Seuil 1972.

Simon, Claude. *La Route des Flandres*. Paris: Les Editions de Minuit 1960.

Socken, Paul G. *Myth and Morality in "Alexandre Chenevert" by Gabrielle Roy.* Frankfurt: Peter Lang 1987.

Tannen, Deborah. "Repetition in Conversation: Toward a Poetics of Talk." *Language* 63, no. 3 (1987): 574–605.

Tétu, Michel. *La Francophonie: histoire, problématique, perspectives*. Montréal: Guérin 1987.

Wittgenstein, Ludwig. *Philosophical Investigations*. Trans. G.E.M. Anscombe. 1945. New York: Macmillan 1968.

Index

absurdity, 92
agent double, 102
A la recherche du temps perdu, 20, 89
Alexandre Chenevert, 5, 35, 41, 50–3, 55–9, 61, 63, 124
Altbekanntheit, 12
"antagonistic" mode, 45, 55, 58, 70, 75, 100, 105, 112, 113
anthology, 5, 8, 16–18, 34, 35, 41
Aphorismen, 10, 25
Aphorismus, 10–12, 33
appropriation, 28–30, 32
archetype, 43, 66, 73, 74, 107
A Room of One's Own, 17
atomization, 91
audience, 63, 75, 96, 113
Aussparung, 27
author, 3, 5, 9–12, 14, 16, 18, 20, 21, 25, 26, 28, 29, 34, 36, 38–40, 43, 47, 49, 50, 53, 55, 61, 63, 64, 71, 81, 89, 96, 105, 107, 109, 113, 114

backgrounding, 21–3, 107, 111
banal, 13, 17, 85, 89, 97
banality, 12, 26, 55, 81
Barthes, Roland, 17, 87
Bennington, Geoffrey, 3, 4, 8, 13, 34, 35, 116
Beutel, A.W., 112
Bevan, David, 93
Biyidi, O., 71
"Black English Vernacular" (BEV), 18, 20
Bonheur d'occasion, 52
The Bridge of Beyond, 76
Burke, Kenneth, 4, 16, 28, 30–2, 106

Cahier d'un retour au pays natal, 71
Les Caractères, 115
categorics, 8, 19, 57, 70, 73
Césaire, Aimé, 71, 75
Cézanne, Paul, 94, 98, 99
chain, 3, 4, 12, 18–20, 26, 41–3, 49, 64, 68, 76, 77, 99, 108
chain of events, 3, 4, 19, 20, 49, 64

Chevrier, Pierre, 39, 40
chiasmus, 27, 45, 85
cinematography, 94, 104, 106, 108, 109
Citadelle, 37, 39, 40
Colette, 7
commonplace, 3, 17, 46, 55, 96
Compagnon, Antoine, 20
concealed aphorisms, 26, 29
consciousness, 5, 23, 29, 43, 56, 61, 80, 81, 84–7, 96, 115
constraints, 115
Courrier Sud, 37, 38

Dällenbach, Lucien, 80, 81, 84
define, 4, 8, 11, 12, 15, 18, 26, 29, 65, 66, 85
definition of aphorism, 11
degré zéro, 17, 29, 87
Delson-Karan, Myrna, 50
Derrida, Jacques, 13, 28, 35, 75
Le Désert mauve, 115
Deutsches Wörterbuch, 14
diachronic, 11

Die fröhliche Wissenschaft, 46

discourse, 4, 7, 8, 10, 12–14, 17, 18, 20, 21, 23, 24, 29, 31, 34, 35, 37, 44, 51, 56, 69, 72–5, 83, 84, 97, 98, 110, 111, 113, 116

discourse function, 4

disguised aphorisms, 40, 49, 55

"La Disparition élocutoire du poète," 102

drama, 11, 13, 59, 84

durative, 22–4, 42, 54, 83

Ecrits de guerre, 37

editorial commentary, 54, 93

eighteenth century, 9, 77

Einfall, 34

element of surprise, 26

embedding, 9, 10, 34, 40, 41, 48

en abyme, 81, 84, 95, 144

English, 18, 19, 27, 55

epigram, 8

essay, 16, 18, 30, 39, 41, 42, 44, 50, 51, 94, 95, 98, 102–4

essayistic, 20, 23, 34, 41, 42, 49, 63, 104, 106, 110, 112

Estang, Luc, 38, 39

eternal return, 70, 75

evaluation, 19–21, 23, 43, 53, 56, 72, 82–4, 94, 100, 103, 105, 111

exaggeration, 25

L'Exemple de Cézanne, 94

feminist, 59

Fielding, Henry, 9

Flaubert, Gustave, 112, 114

foregrounding, 21–3, 107

Fowler, Carolyn, 10, 20, 62–5, 67, 68

Fowler, Roger, 9

France, 6, 33

francophone, 3, 6, 9, 12, 17, 19, 28, 32, 34, 49, 55, 60, 71, 75, 101, 112–14, 116

francophonie, 6

French, 3–5, 7, 8, 10, 11, 14, 22, 24, 25, 28, 32–4, 45, 49, 51, 55, 58, 59, 71, 77, 86, 96–8, 112–14, 116

Freudian, 30, 35

function of aphorism, 4, 7, 8, 12, 14–16, 18, 28, 33, 36, 39, 44, 75, 76, 83, 111, 112, 114

genre, 4, 8–14, 17, 18, 24, 31, 39, 46, 51, 57, 61, 71, 95, 111–13, 125

German, 4, 5, 10, 11, 14, 27, 29, 32, 33, 37, 38, 45, 47, 58, 70

Germany, 33

Gide, André, 7, 23, 39

Gouverneurs de la rosée, 5, 62, 63, 66, 67, 69, 70, 72

grammatical, 19, 73

Grasset, 21

Gray, Richard T., 10, 28, 31–3, 36, 45

Greiner, Ulrich, 25

Gross, John, 9, 15–17, 32, 113

Hamlet, 104, 144

Hébert, Anne, 115

Heidegger, Martin, 29, 30

Heidenreich, Rosmarin, 101, 102

hermeneutics, 4, 28–32, 60, 113

Hopper, Paul, 4, 18, 21, 22, 83

humanism, 5, 38, 48–51, 59

humanist, 39, 49, 50, 59, 60, 68, 90

Humphries, Jefferson, 3, 4, 8, 24

Husserl, Edmund, 29

hyperbole, 25, 46, 57, 84, 114

idiosyncratic, 5, 16, 17, 23, 28, 38, 59, 89, 94, 98, 111

L'Immoraliste, 8, 23

indecipherability, 36, 102

indeterminacy, 4, 5, 28, 80, 102, 103

interpretation, 29, 51, 63, 100, 113

intertext, 107, 112, 113

involuntary memory, 89

ironic, 38, 56, 57, 76

irony, 56–9, 61, 75, 103, 114, 116

iterative, 22–4, 42, 83

La Jalousie, 115

Jean-Luc Persécuté, 99

Joyce, James, 114

Kadish, Doris, 79

Kafka, Franz, 28, 31

Kafka's Aphorism, 10

Kamouraska, 115

Labov, William, 4, 18–21, 43, 52, 81–3, 96

La Bruyère, Jean de, 33, 58, 75

Lacan, Jacques, 28

Language and the Inner City, 18

language games, 21

"laying down the law," 9

Lewis, Paula Gilbert, 50

lexicon, 13, 14, 48, 73, 83, 97

lieu commun, 26, 46, 65

Life and Work of Jacques Roumain, 62

Linguistics and the Novel, 9

"Literature as Equipment for Living," 30

Loubère, J.A.E., 79, 80

Madame Bovary, 31, 113

Marx, Karl, 63, 68, 70, 88

Mautner, Franz, 11, 18
maxim, 3, 8, 15, 26, 32–5, 46
May, Cedric, 101
metalingual, 83
metaphor, 28, 39, 43, 74, 106
metaphysics, 5, 50, 65, 67, 87, 95
mise en abyme, 81, 144
moralistes, 7, 25, 32, 33, 45, 49, 112, 114
moralizing, 100, 114, 115
morphology, 22–4, 97

narrated chain of events, 3, 4, 49, 64
narration, 21, 23, 24, 34, 37, 39–44, 49, 54, 55, 64, 72, 73, 76, 79, 81, 82, 84, 95, 96, 100, 104, 105, 107, 111, 113, 116
narrative, 4, 5, 7, 9, 10, 17–24, 31, 34–6, 39–41, 43, 44, 49, 51–4, 56, 61, 62, 65, 66, 70, 72, 73, 76, 77, 79–81, 83, 84, 86, 89, 96, 97, 103, 104, 107, 112, 113, 115
narratology, 18, 24, 36, 40, 43, 44, 53, 63, 72, 77, 81, 95, 96, 104, 107
narrator, 19, 20, 23, 38, 43, 44, 47, 48, 53, 63–5, 78, 83, 85, 89, 94–6
national literatures, 8, 34, 112
La Nausée, 7
Neige noire, 5, 101, 102, 104–8, 143
Nelligan, Emile, 107
neologism, 27
New Critics, 28, 113
new novelists, 94
Nietzsche, Friedrich, 5, 9, 15, 34, 37, 38, 45–8, 63, 64, 68–70, 105, 106, 112, 114
nihilistic, 106

nothingness, 91, 98
nouveau roman, 5, 82, 116

Oedipus, 109
Ollendorff (publishers), 21, 23
open-endedness, 26
Ormerod, Beverly, 71, 73–6
overstated, 86, 113
The Oxford Book of Aphorisms, 15, 27
oxymoron, 28, 56

Pascal, Blaise, 33, 37, 45, 70, 95, 121, 122
passé simple, 7, 22–4
Pélissier, Georges, 39
La Peste, 115
phenomenology, 29
photography, 103
poetry, 3, 12, 13, 16, 39, 44
pointe, 14, 26, 56, 116
point of the narrative, 19, 72
Ponge, Francis, 44
The Postwar Novel in Canada, 101
Présence de la mort, 5, 93–5, 97–100
present tense, 7, 9, 17, 20, 22, 23, 34, 54, 83, 104, 107
preterit, 19, 22, 23, 82
La Princesse de Clèves, 7
Prochain épisode, 103
procrustean bed, 114
progress, 68, 88
prose, 3, 7–13, 15, 18, 51, 93, 95, 103, 110, 112
Prose Observations, 15
Proust, Marcel, 7, 20, 21, 23, 61, 89, 99
proverb, 8, 9, 16, 18, 32, 46, 63, 113
punctual, 22, 24

Québec, 60, 104, 105, 107, 144

Rader, Margaret, 13
Ramuz, C.F., 5, 72, 93–100
récit, 19, 20, 23, 39, 41, 42, 53
referentiality, 14, 18, 24, 26, 27, 54, 87, 107, 114
réflexion, 33
reflexivity, 83, 115
Les Relations humaines dans l'œuvre de Saint-Exupéry, 47
Renaud, Philippe, 93
Renault, Alain, 59
reported events, 22, 39, 42, 43, 64, 72, 112
reporting, 19, 20, 41, 42, 49, 82, 83, 96
ressentiment, 69
reste, 52, 97, 108, 125, 126, 131, 142, 143
Ricard, François, 51, 59
Ricœur, Paul, 5, 28–31, 106
Rodegem, François, 8
La Route des Flandres, 5, 35, 36, 79–81, 84, 86, 87, 91, 104, 136
Roy, Gabrielle, 5, 35, 41, 49–61, 63
rubric, 27, 75, 105
rubrics, 35

Saint-Exupéry, Antoine de, 5, 23, 36–41, 43, 45–51, 53, 58, 104, 114
Sarraute, Nathalie, 115
Sartre, Jean-Paul, 7, 88, 99
Schlusspointe, 27, 106
Schwarz-Bart, Simone, 5, 71, 72, 74, 75, 76, 77
segment, 14, 23, 41, 42, 72, 104
selfhood, 47, 59, 103, 107
sentence, 7–9, 12, 14–17, 23, 35, 37, 40, 41, 45, 49, 72, 74–7, 84, 86, 97, 106, 107, 115
sententiousness, 3, 4, 8, 13, 64, 96

Shek, B.-Z., 51, 52
signified, 15, 106, 114
signifier, 14, 15, 17, 106
signposts, 21, 103, 115
simile, 28
Simon, Claude, 72, 80–92, 106
Simon's, 5, 35, 36, 79, 104
Smart, Patricia, 102
Socken, Paul, 50–3, 59, 61
"Soir d'hiver," 107
spoken discourse, 74
"stamp and style" of an author, 36
Stephenson, R.H., 12
story-line, 21
style, 16, 27, 32, 36–8, 45, 58, 95, 97, 103, 105, 112
subgenre, 4, 111
superlatives, 25, 46, 86, 105, 114

"Taille de l'homme," 95
taxonomy, 8, 20, 33
teleological, 88
Le Temps retrouvé, 20
tendresse, 38, 59
tense, 7, 9, 17, 19, 20, 22–4, 34, 35, 40, 49, 54, 81, 83, 98, 104, 107
Terre des Hommes, 5, 23, 36, 37, 39, 40, 42, 45–7, 49–51, 56, 58, 104
terseness, 16, 32, 40, 45, 57, 73, 81, 95
Tétu, Michel, 6
text, 5, 6, 9, 11, 14, 18, 23–6, 28–32, 34–7, 39–41, 43, 44, 46–9, 51–61, 64, 66, 67, 71, 73–7, 79–81, 83–7, 90–2, 94–8, 102–4, 106–15
"Le Texte ou le silence marginal," 103
textual, 5, 18, 25, 29, 84, 102, 114, 115
timeless, 17, 20, 23, 24, 35, 54
Tom Jones, 9, 34
topic, 10, 36, 42, 46, 62, 65, 69, 84–6, 106, 108, 109
topicality, 84
Tougas, Gérard, 51
truth, 9, 15, 20, 27, 34, 48, 60, 91, 116
twentieth century, 3, 19, 34, 113, 116
Twilight of the Idols, 15
"type situations," 30

typology, 11, 30

Übermensch, 70
Überrumpelung, 27
Überspitzung, 25, 26
understatement, 26
universalizing, 20, 42, 81, 88, 90

Verhaltensregeln, 33
Verrätselung, 27
verweisen, 13, 14
La Volonté de puissance, 38

Western civilization, 44, 54, 59, 68, 90, 112
will to power, 53
Wittgenstein, Ludwig, 21, 30
"world of the text," 28, 29, 31, 32, 46, 58, 67, 76, 87, 98, 106
Wörterbuch der philosophischen Begriffe, 112
written discourse, 13, 73, 113

Zarathustra, 37, 64, 69
zeugma, 28, 56
Zur Genealogie der Moral, 69